INTO DEEP WATER

THE EXPERIENCE OF CURATES
IN THE CHURCH OF ENGLAND

NEIL BURGESS

Kevin Mayhew

First published in 1998 by
KEVIN MAYHEW LTD
Rattlesden
Bury St Edmunds
Suffolk IP30 0SZ

0 1 2 3 4 5 6 7 8 9

ISBN 1 84003 187 5
Catalogue No 1500190

Cover photograph reproduced courtesy
of SuperStock, London
Cover design by Jaquetta Sergeant
Typesetting by Louise Selfe
Printed and bound in Great Britain

CONTENTS

This book is dedicated to all those who were students at Lincoln Theological College between 1987 and 1996 and now work in the ministries of the Methodist and Anglican Churches.

FOREWORD

Dr Neil Burgess' study of curates and their work is long over-due. It is valuable because it allows the people he interviewed to talk about their experiences in their own words, and the reader is invited to view events through these curates' eyes. There is human interest here which engages the reader and asks them to pay attention to the people who are speaking.

What the curates say about their ministries, their lives after ordination and their hopes and fears for the future is often disturbing. Too many of them have found that ministry, which is never easy, has been made more difficult by being asked to work with clergy who seem unable to fulfil even the most basic commitments of a trainer let alone a colleague. No one who is concerned for the future of the Church and its ministry can afford to ignore what is said here.

Any book which makes unwelcome or disturbing claims about the Church's ministry will provoke protests or opposi-tion. However, since this book is the outcome of some care-ful research among curates, it simply asks any who wish to challenge its evidence or conclusions to come up with equally well-researched information of their own.

Dr Burgess also offers some suggestions of how the present situation can be remedied. Many of his proposals either reflect accepted practice in other jobs, or else build upon existing practice in the churches. While some may be unwilling to accept what is proposed, leaving things as they are does not seem to be a constructive option.

I hope this book will be read carefully and feel it will help forward a debate about ministry in the Church today.

It is the aim of all, within the Church, who are concerned about quality ministry which serves the whole community, to ensure it is founded on good practice.

Rt Revd Alan Morgan, Bishop of Sherwood
Former Chair of the Ministry Committee, Diocese of Southwell

NOTE ON QUOTATIONS

This book is written around verbatim quotations from taped conversations with curates in the Church of England. This method has been used to convey, as far as possible within a continuous text, the sense of what the people concerned actually said. Some editing has been employed in order to remove the repetition, asides, false starts and unfinished sentences which inevitably occur in speech. Nevertheless, some quotations may not read as well as they would if written down in the first instance, but it is hoped that any difficulty this causes will be acceptable in the interests of authenticity.

CHAPTER 1

Great expectations? Setting the scene for the research

> What a curious institution [the Church] is! It's so open to abuse, of twisting theology to add to one's own sense of inadequacy and guilt and so rarely affirming; extraordinarily pastorally insensitive sometimes . . . the Church has struck me [often] as being an uncaring, disinterested institution . . . [but there are also] the great joys of the Church; I don't want to lose sight of that. I love the Church with a passion . . . which surprises me. I've nowhere else to go; the Church of England's my home and I love it, but it drives me wild!

This book is an account of people and their work. The people are ordained ministers of the Church of England and their work is that which they do as curates, at the start of their ministerial careers. All twenty people whose experiences are discussed here work in full-time, paid ministry; all were trained for ordination at Lincoln Theological College and were ordained as Deacons between 1989 and 1994. This apart, they are a diverse group, men and women aged from their mid-twenties to late forties, from differing backgrounds, having worked at a variety of jobs before ordination and now in dioceses all over England. They are anonymous because it was agreed before they were interviewed that nothing would be published which would positively identify them. It is unfortunate if readers find this annoying, but without this assurance of anonymity they would have been unwilling to be as open and candid as they were about their experiences.

Twenty may seem a very small survey group upon which to base any conclusions about ministry in a Church with almost 10,000 clergy. A small sample to be interviewed at some length, two hours each, was decided upon rather than a larger sample to be approached through a questionnaire since I sensed that greater justice could be done to the complexities of their experiences in this way. As a result of this project I now have forty hours of audio tape in which clergy tell of their experiences, hopes and fears. However, other, wider-ranging surveys have been undertaken into this question which substantially reinforce the conclusions of my own research; these are discussed briefly in Appendix 3.

The book is intended to be a human document, concerned first of all with people. I have therefore given a good deal of space to verbatim quotations from the interviews, by which my anonymous respondents can be allowed to speak for themselves. It would be dishonest to claim that what is presented has not gone through a process of editing or selection; but I am struck by just how representative are many of the comments and experiences recorded here. Since completing the first half of the research in the summer of 1994 I published an article in the *British Journal of Theological Education*[1] outlining my initial findings. I subsequently presented a short paper at the annual conference of the British & Irish Association for Practical Theology in Oxford in 1996 in which I discussed my work with delegates, many of whom work either in training candidates for ministry in the churches or in in-service training. A significant number of people responded to both these presentations by indicating not only their awareness of the issues raised, but also the extent to which their own careers in churches of different denominations reflected those of my interviewees. Such comments suggest that these twenty anonymous ministers may speak not only for curates but also of the formative experiences of many longer-serving clergy in the Church of England and other traditions.

There are good theological reasons for this focus on people. As well as being created in the image and likeness of God, people are the most significant tangible assets the churches have – in this world at least. The teaching of Jesus places a high value on people, to the extent of seeing their lives and needs as more pressing than the hallowed traditions of Israel.[2] Like the prophets, he argues that the ways in which people are treated, for good or ill, are one of the tests of the righteousness of the nation. It is not fanciful, therefore, to suggest that the ways in which the churches treat the people they count as members and ministers is a significant test of their institutional grasp of the gospel. Institutions are much more than the sum of the people of which they are composed; they give form, direction and meaning to lives and embody the understandings by which people live and interpret the world. So any study like this, even if it starts with individuals, must also have an institutional dimension. To ignore this would be naïve about the processes which shape people's lives and hopes.

The last point is worth stressing because there is evidence that, within the Church of England at least, there is a strong culture which discounts the experience and opinions of those who are either candidates for ordination or newly ordained. Professor Leslie Francis cites examples of episcopal criticisms directed towards a piece of participant-observation research he conducted in the 1980s, using ordinands as observers.[3] One bishop commented that, 'ordinands are notoriously difficult to please', while another wrote that the observers

> . . . reveal themselves as censorious, imperceptive, humourless and unloving. But, never mind; given time and good training vicars they will be eventually licked into shape.

Similarly with curates. Charles Forder, whose book on the work of ministry has found its way on to many clergy bookshelves since it was first published in 1946, discusses curates as much in terms of potential threats to their incumbents as assets, commenting:

> Curates are usually so full of life, enthusiasm and zeal that they almost inevitably think they can do the job better than the parish priest, who is sure to have gained a mature cautiousness.[4]

Whether they are seen as unloving or over-zealous, there is a sense that ordinands' and curates' opinions are easily dismissed, while there seems real menace in the episcopal hope that they can be 'licked into shape'. My own view is that it is precisely their freshness of viewpoint that makes their observations worth listening to. Outsiders and newcomers have a vital role in any organisation because they have not internalised the institutional culture or learned to lower their expectations to the level of the *status quo*. They are the ones who see most clearly whether the emperor has any clothes and have not learned to keep their observations to themselves, even if this can be uncomfortable. On the other hand, in conducting these interviews I was often impressed by the curates' moderation and self-criticism. When they made criticisms of others they were frequently at pains to search for extenuating circumstances and to affirm their essential commitment to people and Church.

A PERSONAL VIEW

It is important at this point to declare some of my own interests and commitments in this research. I was ordained deacon in the Church of England in 1977 and worked in parish ministry in the north Midlands for ten years. In 1987 I was appointed Director of Pastoral Studies at Lincoln Theological College and it was there that I first met and taught those whom later I interviewed. Some were my tutorial students, some were people with whom I struck up a friendship because we found common interests or outlooks on life. All were people with ability and a clear dedication to the study of theology in preparation for ministry. It might be claimed that such a prior acquaintance undermines the objectivity of my research; I believe though that because I was known to those whom I interviewed there was no need to establish a rapport with them before they would disclose their experiences. They knew my own approaches to ministry from college days, so there was no need to guess my standpoint on issues; equally, I had been able to establish beforehand that these were people whose judgement I trusted and whose self-awareness could be relied upon.

In January 1995, just as I was planning the second round of interviews, the bishops of the Church of England announced that, since numbers of ordination candidates had been falling for some time and there was a substantial over-provision of residential training places, Lincoln would no longer be recognised as a place of training for ordinands. This meant that, along with my colleagues, I would be made redundant at the end of the academic year. However, I was fortunate in finding another post; on 1st July I started work as Director of Clergy Training in the Diocese of Southwell, responsible for in-service training for clergy throughout the diocese and also director of Post-Ordination Training for curates. While this transition has given me a particular viewpoint from which to discuss training for ministry, it has also given me the opportunity to attempt to address some of the issues raised by this research. The period around my appointment also produced a curious sense of *déjà vu*. Between Easter and June I met with the second group of ten interviewees, whose accounts of ministry largely supported the conclusions drawn from the first group the previous year. During July, having started in my new post, I visited most of the curates in the Diocese of Southwell, who independently reinforced the conclusions I was forming from my research. So it was that the first year or so in the new job saw me involved in trying not only to get people moved from unsatisfactory curacies but also revising the Post-Ordination Training structure to try to ensure that such problems did not recur.

A further dimension to my personal involvement in this research is my own experience of two curacies. I have since recognised that what happened to me could be repeated by many other curates, then and since, but at the time it was both worrying and discouraging. In truth, there was little enough structured learning. Initially, I was taught how to conduct rites of passage such as funerals and weddings, and, as I approached ordination as a priest at the end of my first year, how to preside at the Eucharist. My first incumbent also asked to see the text of my early sermons, though as I had preached a good deal before ordination and increasingly used only brief notes, this soon ceased. On the day I was ordained deacon the vicar of another parish in the deanery left to take up a new appointment. The parish comprised a large council housing estate with many funerals, often two or three a week. As soon as my incumbent was satisfied I could do so, I was packed off on my motorcycle to take the funerals. No one ever asked how I was getting on, or what the effects of dealing with so much death and bereavement had on a young man of twenty-four. Indeed, I cannot recall more than a handful of 'staff meetings' for routine planning and discussion, even though the diocesan expectation was that they should happen weekly. Instead I was expected to come to the rectory each day, be given a job to do and come back for more when I had finished. In time I began to find projects of my own, but these were never discussed. But around every two months I would be summoned to bring my fountain pen, filled with black ink, to the rectory; under my colleague's close supervision I would sign my name against the immaculately written entries in the service register, red for Sundays and major Saints' days, black for the rest, itemising the services I had conducted since the last signing.

Initially my second curacy looked more promising, but eleven months after arriving, my rector moved to take up another appointment. I was left 'acting in charge' for almost two years, though this hardly affected the training process as I had grown accustomed to finding out things for myself and the church members were exceptionally supportive. In 1982, I became vicar of two districts in a team ministry, having picked up a good many scraps of information and experience along the way; but there was no sense that, after five years of ordained ministry and two incumbents, I had really been *trained*, or made to examine my assumptions at all closely.

I can now write about this with a measure of equanimity and I do so not to criticise my former colleagues but to affirm that, twenty years later, I am aware that curates are still treated in much the same way in dioceses up and down the country. In my daily work I am occasionally upbraided by clergy with curates who assure me that they have no time to talk with their colleagues, much less offer them training or assess their progress. This leads me to believe that twenty years hence the situation will still be unchanged unless people with power in the Church revise their expectations of what is needed and what is possible.

GREAT EXPECTATIONS?

Expectation does seem to be a key to much of what is discussed in this book. Anyone embarking on a new job does so with some measure of expectation. Often this is positive and hopeful, if only because this is a natural reinforcement of the decision to make the change; where people feel forced by circumstances or other people's decisions to take a job, they may be far less optimistic. When taking up a new career, having retrained after years of working at something else, these expectations may be all the more significant. In the case of newly ordained clergy there is a further layer, often discussed as a sense of vocation or commitment to a set of values or ideals; that, in offering themselves to God through the ordained ministry of the Church, they expect to find the Church supportive of their actions and sustaining in its acceptance of them. Curates are not the only people with expectations, of course. Their families harbour expectations of what this step will mean for their spouse or children. They may see new possibilities and hopes ahead; or may be apprehensive of living in an area where they might feel out of place or of being pushed into a role they do not want, for instance as the 'curate's wife'.

New colleagues also have expectations of curates, hoping that here is someone to do the visiting for which they lack the time, attract new churchgoers, or heal old rifts in the congregation. In parishes where there are other authorised and ordained ministers beside the incumbent, there may be a sense of apprehension that the newcomer may take over some functions which others have previously exercised; a good many lay readers have in this way been displaced by curates, whether the latter realised what was happening or not. On the other hand, some incumbents see the arrival of a curate as a sign that the bishop has favoured or honoured them in some way, perhaps even marked them for 'higher things' in the future. Curates can be ecclesiastical status-symbols and this causes problems if for some reason the incumbent is not given a new curate when the last one leaves.

Church members may similarly harbour a range of expectations about a new curate. The oft-quoted hope that they will be 'good with children and young people' may be reinforced if they have young children of their own. Some people hope for a curate who is unlike the incumbent; others may expect the newcomer to be of the same mind as not only their senior colleague but the prominent groups in the congregation. If there have been curates in the past, the newcomer may find a role sketched out for them which they may or may not welcome. Until recently there has been an expectation that curates will be younger than their incumbents, but with an increasing number of older ordinands this is no longer necessarily the case. This can also create conflicts of expectation: the younger incumbent has more ministerial experience than the older curate, but the curate may have a wider experience of the world of work in which the congregation are located. More recently still, women have challenged some of the assumptions about curates, who before 1987 would have been exclusively male. A sidelight on this has been the emergence of the 'clergy husband', who seems to have fewer expectations laid upon him than 'clergy wives' did, at least in the past.

Enough has been said so far to indicate the breadth of expectations and the plurality of their sources. Some may seem reasonable enough; others occupy the ill-charted ground between reality and pure fantasy. It seems fair enough to expect that curates will be willing and able to work alongside other people, share responsibilities and accountability, pull their weight in the day-to-day work of ministry, be part of a Christian community and not neglect their families. Curates are entitled to expect their share of respect as human beings, Christians and colleagues, entitled to equitable treatment over tasks to be done, leisure to be enjoyed and a reasonable standard of housing and remuneration. They are also entitled to expect a proper and methodical training to equip them not only for their present work but also for future responsibilities, in which their skills can be recognised and developed and in which they can continue to test the nature and scope of their calling. Nevertheless the findings of this research indicate that even these elementary expectations are not always being met.

Other expectations are both more complex and to some extent dependent upon the basic ones. The curates whom I interviewed for this study had a strong sense of wanting to be stretched by their work in ministry, to have their resolve and abilities put to the test. This desire owes much to centuries of Christian thought, often expressed through liturgy, devotion and personal piety, about the nature of vocation in the name of one who gave his life for the redemption of the world. These ideas are brought home to candidates for ordained ministry through a lengthy process of selection, training and eventually ordination itself, in which the demands of the calling are described as beyond human capacity without the empowering grace of God. But it is also part of a very human desire to find some assurance, however passing or apparently insignificant, that someone who has made such a change in the pattern of their life has not been mistaken in so doing. It is also in the nature of much of the thinking about vocation that people expect the work of ministry to be theologically and religiously meaningful; that being a minister is an integral, contributory part of one's Christian life. This desire might be powerful enough for a single person, but for married people there is a further sense of responsibility for the upheaval caused to one's partner and children in giving up a job, possibly a family home, and moving to college, only to have to repeat the upheaval two or three years later on ordination. Several of those interviewed made it clear that they felt, at some time in their early years, that they had made a mistake by being ordained and had inflicted this mistake on their families as well as themselves. Some were also clear that they felt their Christian faith to be compromised by the work they were doing, or the person they were expected to be.

INTRODUCING THE CURATES

Although it was always the intention to protect the anonymity of the interviewees, it is useful to give some information about them to reinforce the findings of the research. As noted earlier, all twenty were students at Lincoln Theological College in the late 1980s and early 1990s, the most recently ordained having been made deacon in 1994. At the time of being interviewed the youngest was 26 and the eldest 49. Fifteen were married, thirteen men and two women, ten with children and another two with children expected during the year; the single people comprised four women and one man.

They had served, or were serving, their curacies in fifteen dioceses throughout England, three in the Province of York and twelve in the Province of Canterbury. At the time of being interviewed six had moved from their first curacies and three more were on the point of doing so.

Before commencing training, sixteen respondents had gained at least one first degree. Six had degrees in Theology, the others being in Botany, Business Studies, Classics, Commerce, General Studies, Geography, History, Management Studies and Physics. Two had gained higher degrees. Eleven had gained one or more professional qualifications, and all but one had worked in a variety of careers before coming into ordination training, including education, engineering, the health service, business management, computers, public transport, social work and the law.

The interviewees were asked to indicate what work they thought they might have been doing had they not been ordained. Twelve people said they were reasonably confident that their previous careers would have continued to offer them opportunities for further responsibility and promotion. The others were either less certain of what they wanted to do, or felt that they were free to explore a number of future career options. This question was originally included in the research to see how what they were doing in ministry might compare with what might have been, a question which people could reasonably ask themselves after a career shift; but also because there have been suggestions that offering for ordination might be a way of moving off a 'career plateau', or the means of escaping from a job which either offered few prospects or was unsatisfying. The latter point reveals an expectation of people having 'jobs for life', spending all their working lives in one occupation, or even working for one employer. The responses of the eight reflect a different ethos where the idea of such continuity of employment is not one of the taken-for-granted assumptions of life. But this changing social reality also questions some long-held assumptions about

Christian vocation. In an age of life-long careers, a call to ordained ministry perhaps needed to be understood as a radical dislocation, something from God which could not be resisted. After ordination, ministry became a new 'career for life'. In times of more fluid employment, ordination may become one of a number of career-change options which Christians can consider rationally at different points in their working lifetime. If they pursue it, this too may be for a period, after which they work at something else. This does not reduce the sense which people may have that they are 'truly called'; but it does suggest that the language used to describe the calling and the expectations of where it might lead may need fundamental re-thinking. Later, in Chapter 5, it will be clear that some of the curates felt that even the Church was a somewhat precarious employer in modern times and that future work outside of its full-time paid ministry could not be ruled out.

During their time at Lincoln the interviewees had under-taken different courses. The six Theology graduates and a further six, who were over the age of thirty when they started training, undertook two-year courses. The other seven worked on the three-year Bachelor of Theology degree course run jointly between the College and the University of Nottingham. This distribution between different training courses roughly reflects the relative numbers of students undertaking the courses in the period from 1987 to 1994.

Respondents were also asked about their religious allegiances, the kinds of churches to which they had belonged and whether they had held any positions of responsibility in the churches in the ten years before beginning training. Sixteen considered themselves to have been Christians all their lives or from childhood, of whom six had been members of other Christian denominations, all Free Church, before becoming Anglicans. The others indicated that they considered that they had been Christians for less than their lifetimes, two having been baptised by total immersion as teenagers, though they all saw themselves as having been Christian for longer than they had not. No one identified themselves as having been an adherent of another faith before becoming a Christian. They described the churches they had attended prior to coming to Lincoln as a mixture of 'fairly Anglican Catholic but not rigid'; 'middle-of-the-road to catholic'; 'Anglo-Catholic, urban, mixed race'; 'suburban C of E'; 'liberal in theology; "low" rather than "high" in liturgy'; 'fairly broad-based, low C of E'; 'middle to high'; 'liberal Catholic Anglican with a radical priest'; 'traditional Anglican parish church'; 'broad in churchmanship'; 'UPA parish . . . lively and friendly'; and 'UPA inner city – wooden liberal catholic liturgy in a wooden breeze-block church'. Before starting ordination training one had been a churchwarden, three were authorised local lay ministers, another was 'officially known as the Honorary Lay Pastoral Assistant', and others were licensed to adminis-ter the chalice at communion. In the ten years before the start of training ten had been involved in Sunday Schools or youth work, eleven had been members of parochial church councils and others had held lay offices in Free Churches or had been members of Anglican deanery synods, sacristans, choristers, housegroup and study group leaders.

The interviewees were also asked to describe who, either singly or in a group, had been most influential in helping them think about ordination. Fifteen mentioned clergy whom they had known, three mentioning people they had met during childhood or while still at school. Eight also mentioned laypeople, including members of a religious community, a Reader at the church they attended, other church members, students at university or colleagues at work, all of whom had either recognised potential for ministry or else helped them think through the questions involved in ordination. Two mentioned that other family members had been a Free Church minister, or a lay preacher, and two others commented that their spouses had offered support and encouragement. No one described a sudden sense that this was what God was asking them to do, but rather that it was a very long process of thought, prayer and exploration.

This very brief summary of interviewees' self-descriptions indicates that most if not all were of a broadly educated middle-class background by the time they came to Lincoln, having been long-term if not life-long Christians and having a fair degree of experience of involvement with the organisation of the churches in which they had been members. Those churches had tended to be within the broad centre-stage of Anglicanism, tending towards the 'high church' rather than evangelical end of the spectrum. As such they were broadly typical of many of the students who had passed through the College over the previous three decades, and of many other Anglican clergy more generally. The only obvious difference between the women and the men was that women were more likely to be single. As noted earlier, they were all people of ability and with personal characteristics which would be expected to stand them in good stead in their future ministries. It is now time to discover how they fared as they embarked on their work as clergy.

NOTES

1 Neil Burgess, 'Training in the Early Years of Ministry: a Cause for Concern?' in *British Journal of Theological Education,* vol. 8, no. 1 (spring 1996), pp. 27-32.

2 e.g. Mark 2:27: 'the Sabbath was made for the people, not the people for the Sabbath'.

3 Leslie Francis, *ChurchWatch: Christianity in the Countryside*, London, SPCK (1996), p. 23.

4 Charles Forder, *The Parish Priest at Work,* London, SPCK (1946), second edition 1964, p. 50.

CHAPTER 2

Finding a job

My whole experience of my first few years in ministry changed me an awful lot; it changed my whole theology, really, and my understanding of mission and what I'm about as a person.

OFFICIAL EXPECTATIONS

One feature of the Church of England which often provokes comment from people in other occupations is that it has no personnel department. All appointments of clergy for parishes and diocesan staff, apart from secretaries and cleaners in the diocesan offices, pass through the Bishop's Staff, a group comprising the diocesan and suffragan bishops, the archdeacons and, often, some of the other senior staff in the diocese such as the dean of the cathedral. In the case of curates starting in ministry there are two interconnected processes to be arranged. The first is their ordination, by which they are admitted to Holy Orders as deacons; the second is their appointment and licensing to a post in the diocese, usually a parish but occasionally to a hospital, school or university chaplaincy. Because curates are not placed in sole pastoral charge in their first appointment there is a need to select a job for them in which they will work with a person who can be relied upon to train them in their early years – the Training Incumbent. In recent years the House of Bishops in the Church of England has decided that no one should be given pastoral charge of their own, i.e. be made an incumbent, before completing four years of ministry after being made deacon; in reality this appointment is often made during their fourth year of ministry. Also, during the first three years of ministry all curates are expected to participate in a diocesan process of Post-Ordination Training (POT) which attempts to offer training to develop their skills and awareness in ministry.

This chapter sets out to discuss the expectations which the dioceses have of this process and then takes in some of the comments which the interviewees made about finding their first job and of their earliest memories of working there. In my original research in 1994 I went to interview the Diocesan Directors of Ordinands (DDOs) in three dioceses, Durham, Peterborough and Sheffield, and some of their observations are included here. Since then, as explained in Chapter 1, I have become responsible for part of this process, as Director of Clergy Training, in the Diocese of Southwell. What follows, although based on experiences and discussions in four dioceses, is largely typical of much of the practice throughout the Church of England.

THE PROCESS OF IDENTIFYING A JOB
(LARGELY FROM THE DIOCESAN VIEWPOINT)

Immediately prior to their ordination, candidates for ministry undergo a period of academic and practical training. This can take place either in a residential college, like Lincoln, where students and their families come from all over the country to live for two or three years; or through a non-residential training course, when people continue to live in their own homes and work at their lay careers while pursuing a three-year training which is focused on evening study classes and residential weekends. By its nature non-residential training is particularly suited to the needs of those who wish to be ordained as unpaid clergy (NSMs) and continue to earn their living in another job, though people preparing for full-time ministry occasionally train in this way too. Non-residential courses are arranged on a regional basis to make travel to teaching centres manageable.

Before becoming a candidate for ordination, women and men must attend a selection conference, a series of which are organised around the country every year by the Advisory Board of Ministry (ABM), the central body in the Church of England which oversees selection and training for ministry. If the selectors consider a person has the potential for ministry they are 'recommended for training' – no guarantees are made about ordination – and the training agency (college or course) is thereafter expected to make reports on their progress and suitability to the diocese which sponsors them for ordination as they proceed through training. By the time their training is coming to an end there should therefore be a substantial body of material available to the sponsoring diocese indicating the kinds of people they are and their strengths and weaknesses. To this information can be added the observations the DDO has formed of them from the time they first approached the diocese to talk about ordination.

Ordinands' training courses end in June of each year, with ordinations in late June/early July (Petertide) or late September (Michaelmas). People entering full-time ministry are generally ordained at Petertide, Michaelmas ordinations, where they exist, tending to be for NSMs. Ordination dates are the fixed point from which other dates are calculated, so around a year beforehand thought begins to be given about which parishes might have curates from the following ordination and who might be considered for each. In some dioceses this happens even earlier, eighteen months or so in advance. Before even this happens, dioceses receive central notification of how many full-time curates' posts they will be allowed as part of their central allocation of clergy in any particular year. The bishop and DDO will be aware of which parishes currently have curates expecting to move to their next post during the year, so decisions have to be made about whether these are to have a new curate; if not, other parishes without a curate at present might be considered for one in order to offer the number of posts the diocese can fill from its allocation.

The second main part of this operation is the ordinands themselves. Many people are sponsored for ordination by the diocese in which they lived at the time of first thinking about it. A majority will wish to be ordained in that diocese, often for family reasons, and a majority of those will work their whole career in their diocese of ordination, particularly if they remain in parish ministry.[1] The DDO will approach each person to ask them what they hope for in a first appointment, especially whether they wish to work in their sponsoring diocese or else be released to look for work elsewhere. Some dioceses, such as Durham, regularly have more ordinands than places because their sponsored candidates include a number of university students, and regularly 'export' ordinands by mutual agreement; others seldom do so, unless there are less places than candidates in a particular year.

Ordinands may have a number of factors to consider in looking for a curacy. High on the list for many are family concerns: where children may go to school, where partners may find work or pursue their present careers, where they may be accessible to elderly parents. Certain types of area may be unacceptable for some families, such as deprived inner cities; children may have special educational needs which are better met in one place than in others. There are also ecclesiastical considerations: some may be reluctant to work in a church with a theological tradition radically different from their own, though others may welcome it. Others look for a church with a number of members similar in age or circumstances to themselves, which again may be connected with family expectations.

The parish and training incumbent must also be considered. In general, parishes below a certain size are unlikely to have curates, not least because there would be insufficient work to justify one. On the other hand, because the first curacy is a time of training, a large parish which simply wanted another member of staff would be equally unacceptable, though such parishes do take on first curates, as the interviews confirm.

There are also practical considerations such as the availability of housing of a suitable standard for the curate and a willingness in the parish to reimburse working expenses in accordance with nationally identified criteria. Similarly, the incumbent who is to work with the curate needs to be capable of doing so effectively, overseeing their training in ministry in the parish and able to support them as they begin their ministerial careers. The nature of their work suggests that training incumbents require certain definite skills – in adult education, the practice of supervision, in creating and sustaining a team of colleagues and in managing their own time and workload. They are the pivotal person in the curate's early years of ministry. Ordinands may have certain expectations of a parish, the parish has certain expectations of a curate and the diocese, through the DDO and the bishop, has expectations of both. It may be impossible, even undesirable, to satisfy all these simultaneously and as the interviews indicate, many ordinands effectively abandon some of their positive expectations in looking for a job anyway. But this need not lead to disaster if the training incumbent is carefully chosen, has the necessary skills, and knows how to apply them.

Unfortunately, this is generally not the case. The choice of training incumbents in many dioceses is often based upon unacceptably vague criteria; these are often defined in terms of generalised expectations which could apply to almost any minister, such as a stable relationship to the parish, a person of spiritual maturity, or willing to learn, or one who is not overburdened with other work. Where certain ministerial skills are stated, such as ability to work with others or communicate their skills in ministry, or give space for a curate to grow, these are rarely if ever defined in ways which can be examined and quantified. What seems to happen is that people are presumed to have certain skills and aptitudes, a calculation often based upon their years in ordained ministry, unless evidence is available to the contrary. Dioceses produce manuals for training incumbents, but these also frequently reflect this vague and generally exhortatory approach. Moreover, clergy still become training incumbents even when they are known from their previous work with curates to be unsuitable. This situation often reflects the observation in Chapter 1 that curates can be ecclesiastical status-symbols, affirming the standing of a senior incumbent in a diocese, gained through long service or the holding of minor honours such as being an honorary canon or a rural dean. Whatever is said, the reality seems to be that bishops and DDOs are reluctant to refuse a curate for these ministers in case they 'cause trouble'.

By no means all training incumbents are unsuitable; there are some good, and a few excellent, priests doing this demanding work, as some of the interviewees indicate. But often this is so *despite* the diocese's selection process, not because of it. The problems are usually at the most basic level; training incumbents who do not allow time to talk to their colleagues, much less plan what they are to be doing, ask how they are getting on and assess their progress and future training needs. Some are simply too busy, or disorganised, to work with a colleague; while there is often an almost complete lack of the necessary educational skill to plan and carry out a training programme. Clergy who have these skills could be discovered straightforwardly by any moderately effective diocesan training programme. That it is not discovered, or not acted upon, is one of the most fundamental weaknesses of the present system and it is the curates who pay the price for this.

THE PROCESS OF GETTING A JOB
(LARGELY FROM THE CURATES' VIEWPOINT)

So far the four principal factors in appointing a curate have been identified: the stipends, the parishes available, the training incumbents and the ordinands. If we were discussing probationer ministers in the Methodist Church, the question of who goes where would at this point be decided by the Stationing

Committee, a central body responsible for ministerial appointments, who, acting on the information gathered, would allocate ordinands to posts throughout the country, in which they would serve their probation of two years before being ordained.[2] In the Church of England it is assumed that ordinands have a free choice of where to work, as long as a diocesan bishop will ordain them and, if full-time, there is a stipend for them. The Methodist system sees the responsibility for deploying ministers as lying with the Connexion, through the Conference, its central decision-making body. The Church of England shifts this to the diocese and the ordinand, the first in offering a post, the second in accepting or declining it.

On the face of it, an ordinand in the Church of England has a good deal of choice about their first appointment (though this is not always the case in other Anglican provinces). In reality this choice is often severely curtailed by several factors. The first is pressure of time; as noted earlier, there are two processes to be arranged, ordination and a job, the first being dependent upon the second. Ordinations happen at fixed points in the year; for people entering full-time ministry, this is within a few weeks of the end of their training. Until they start work, ordinands have no income, their last grant cheque having arrived after Easter; they also have nowhere to live if they have been housed in College accommodation, though there may be some leeway in this, say up to the end of July. It is not possible for most ordinands to allow themselves to be put into this position, especially if they have a partner and children to consider. It is simply not an option to wait a few months beyond the end of term in the hope that a more suitable post will come up.

The second factor has already been noted: ordinands are frequently constrained by family wishes and needs to seek work in a particular diocese. This introduces a third factor, which is that within dioceses there is no open system of finding posts whereby DDOs notify the ordinands of which parishes are seeking curates and then allow them to approach the incumbents, be interviewed and offered the job. Instead, DDOs and bishops draw up lists in which ordinands are provisionally matched to particular parishes. The ordinands are then asked to go and look at the place, meet the incumbent, talk things over and make a decision. If the ordinand and their family and the training incumbent are willing to work together, bishops will generally ratify the appointment. There are no competitive interviews, as would be expected in other professions, and a training incumbent would not be sent more than one ordinand at a time. The DDOs' list is based upon the 'one person, one job' principle; there are no 'spare' parishes above the permitted number of ordinands, and ordinands realise that if they refuse a job there will probably be nothing else for them in that diocese. As one interviewee put it:

> You don't have the opportunity [to look at other jobs in the diocese] it's take it or dump it . . . You don't know if you chuck it out [whether] the other things in the bucket are worse or whether they're going to be ten times better. . . Lack of comparison means you just take things as they are.

The main variation to this is where a job cannot be filled from within a diocese and is then advertised around the training agencies for anyone to apply for it. Again, it is assumed that there will be only one person looking at a post at a time and no competitive interviews. This process is slightly more open, but it can sometimes be difficult for those from outside a diocese to get much background information about a place and its incumbent. The Church of England relies heavily on these unofficial networks and 'bush telegraphs' to communicate information which ought to be written down in a proper job description. But since there is frequently no proper job description, anyone without such information can be at a severe disadvantage.

The fourth factor limiting effective choice is lack of information about the job. Particularly when appointments are made within a diocese, there can be only the sparsest details; I am aware of ordinands who have looked at a post, been offered it, accepted and started work without ever seeing a written statement of their duties, the training they would receive, their conditions of service or a grievance procedure. Such information as may be produced often describes the area, the parish, the church and the accommodation without more than a sentence or two about the actual job – sometimes in a document running to five or six sides of typed A4 paper.

The fifth restriction on choice is the lack either of interviewing skills on the part of the training incumbent; or of an effective monitoring process for appointments in the diocese. The idea of competitive job interviews in the Church of England is relatively recent, certainly for parochial posts; many training incumbents may never have been interviewed themselves before they interview a prospective curate. Even so, there is often very little checking by the DDO or bishop of what has passed between training incumbent and ordinand when they meet; or that even basic information about conditions of service has been produced or made available. Moreover, there is disturbing evidence from this study that DDOs and bishops may actually conceal material information from ordinands looking at curacies, particularly if it relates to problems between the incumbent and a previous curate. One interviewee commented:

> The DDO, working with one of the bishops, had clearly put some thought in [to the appointment]; but having said that, subsequently the DDO said to me, 'Well, we know it's difficult there: there have been problems' . . .

while another was more forthright:

> I think I was told a lot of garbage by the bishop about the parish . . . like 'The vicar is the best training

> incumbent we have in the diocese'. Well, the last
> time I went to see [the bishop] he said, 'How are
> things with - - - then? Are you still on speaking
> terms?' I gave a very wishy-washy answer . . . and
> he said, 'Well, I couldn't work with him, you know.'

It is in this process of matching ordinands to jobs that the
deficiencies in selecting training incumbents begin seriously
to affect the workings of the system. People who frequently lack
the skills of training, teamwork and interviewing are expected
to interview and select colleagues for whose training they
will be responsible. This is done in a system which, although
apparently offering choice, actually places severe structural
restrictions on that choice for most ordinands. Training
incumbents are not without responsibility for this situation.
They could demand proper training, or avail themselves of
what was on offer; while there is a suspicion that a system
which nominated more parishes than ordinands would be
unpopular with some training incumbents who would have
to interview several candidates and might not appoint any of
them. But the major responsibility for the deficiencies of the
process lies elsewhere: with the bishops and diocesan staffs
who set up and perpetuate the system, despite the evidence
of its shortcomings.

PUTTING EXPECTATIONS TO THE TEST

So how did the interviewees get on in finding their first jobs?
They were asked their reasons for choosing the curacy and
whether they felt their reasons and expectations were fulfilled
in the light of experience. Several commented on the difficulties
of deciding exactly what the job was about. As one person
put it:

> . . . because it was all new, just absorbing information
> and then trying to process it was very difficult . . .

you just got a tremendous range of impressions which it was actually very difficult to make anything of in detail. . . . It's a case of being overwhelmed by impressions and trying to sort out what's significant. . . . You get all these people throwing information at you and you don't know who they are, or where they're coming from or anything. . . . I think probably I did the best thing and went on instinct, and by and large it's worked out OK. . . . People are very optimistic when they tell you about their parishes, I've discovered.

What seemed to be happening for a good many of the interviewees was that the most workable way of coping with the 'information overload' of looking at parishes and housing, talking to training incumbents and parishioners, and so on, was to reverse the normal criteria for selection. Instead of looking for reasons to positively accept the job, many took the view that they would accept it unless they could find reasons for not doing so. This often resulted in accepting the first thing that was offered, not least because they feared that there would be nothing else in the diocese if they declined it. Some were more positive:

The thing that attracted me . . . in the first place was the description of the nature of the working relationships among the clergy team. I recognised early on that was the key . . . they described themselves collaboratively and collegially and it was that language of co-operation, of equals, rather than [the curate] as a spare pair of hands: I had not seen that written elsewhere, although I don't doubt it occurs elsewhere.

Sometimes the choices were very stark and not always presented very sensitively. One woman recalled:

> On the first day of the summer vac at the end of my first year [at college], when I got home I was rung up at eight o'clock in the morning by the person in charge of Diaconal Ministries who said, 'I've got two parishes for you to look at; you've got to tell me which you want to look at first by eleven o'clock this morning. These are the two parishes.'

Some people had clearly gone through the information presented to them carefully and tried to ask probing questions of the people with whom they might be working. One person described how they had changed their minds about a job they were asked to look at, even if the favourable impression did not long survive working there:

> We knew about the parish before [it was offered] . . . and it wasn't a place we'd particularly have chosen. . . . We came looking thinking, 'We're not going to accept this and the vicar's going to be a prat.' . . . I went through [a series of questions] pretty systematically . . . and got the answers I wanted, about collaborative ministry, being free to develop, not being pushed through a sausage machine, and to have supervision in a creative, supportive way and be trained . . . all these things came up right . . . [also] to be valued as a colleague and not just some dog to follow around and be kicked occasionally . . . all the right answers came back . . . So the conversation with the vicar swung [me] round from a definite 'no' to an enthusiastic 'yes'. . . . But I was wrong!

On the other hand three people recalled different kinds of positive feelings about the job they eventually accepted. These are interesting because they point to the need for some working priorities in deciding what constitutes a suitable curacy.

For one person it was clearly their training incumbent:

> I didn't really like the church people terribly much
> . . . I never felt, with some notable exceptions, that
> I ever got to know them or that they ever got to
> know me. They just were not my sort of people and
> I think I knew that before I went. . . . I [decided]
> that the prime reason for going to serve a title was
> the person who was going to train me . . . I was not
> disappointed in that: I got three years of second-
> to-none training . . . we weren't friends, but we
> worked together extremely well.

Another person was more impressed by the congregation:

> I found my vicar wasn't all that helpful . . . in trying
> to help me understand or make some kind of theo-
> logical sense of what I was doing . . . his classic line
> was, 'Oh well, that's ministry, isn't it?' . . . After a
> while I realised there was going to be little real talk
> about what it was all about. . . . When I [first] met
> my future boss . . . he was quite nice, harmless, but
> it never got beyond that . . . [but] the people I met
> were exciting and excited by being part of the
> church.

A third person recalled that:

> I got on well with the vicar, given that I didn't have
> much choice about it . . . when I arrived he was
> very well established, but there was an openness
> about him; he was doing an Open University degree
> . . . so while I was there he was reading all sorts of
> different books and was an interesting person to
> work with: he didn't see everything in terms of
> church, either, and . . . was quite a creative person.
> [Working with him taught me that] things need to

be interlocked; there was no point in doing one thing without being prepared for it to have an influence later on, or even being prepared to catch what comes out of the event . . . there were lots of different ways of belonging. . . . It was a vision of . . . setting up one thing and keeping an eye on what it might lead to, so that the energy isn't wasted.

These observations are significant in pointing to the sometimes sharp choices which people found themselves making in choosing a curacy. A further point of interest is that the people making them were all looking at jobs outside their 'sponsoring diocese' and all considered more than one post before making their final choice. By contrast, the earlier comments suggest that when location or work in a specific diocese is the prime consideration, as it is for a great many ordinands, the more obviously educational considerations take second place. For those willing or able to take a different view, there is still a pragmatic question about whether the training incumbent or the parish is to have priority in their decision. Even so, where, as in the third case, people feel they have little effective choice, the curacy may still be good because the training incumbent is a good person to work with. Here, though, is a qualification; the last person appreciated their training incumbent's wide-ranging interests and these were stimulated from outside of the parish. Overworked clergy are unlikely to allow themselves these stimuli and may restrict rather than expand their curates' outlook and training.

The interviewees who had looked at more than one curacy before deciding on the one where they eventually worked were asked about their impressions of the jobs they declined and their reasons for doing so. There had been some unfortunate experiences:

[I had looked at two other jobs.] In the first, the parish was enormous, on the edge of - - -, and growing at the rate of so-many hundred houses a year. The vicar had only been there six months and . . . might have been a good person to work with . . . [but] it just terrified me, the way the parish was changing so much and I think he was terrified by it; he hadn't begun to cope. . . . The other one, it was his wife – she ran the place; I met . . . the curate . . . and his wife and son; they looked so ill, drained, battered . . . I thought, 'I'm not going to do that to myself.'

Another person:

[In the other place I looked at, things] . . . ended up hinging on housing; they hadn't got a house for a start and they eventually asked us to go and look at one which was totally, utterly unsuitable. There was no study and the Archdeacon was quoted as saying, 'Well, his wife's going to be working . . . and during the day he can work in the dining room and clear up ready to have something to eat in the evening': that was the sort of attitude. But the prime thing . . . was that the incumbent was totally unsuitable. . . . Without going into all the gory details . . . his wife wrote telling me when I would be taking my summer holidays . . . and [he] was violently against the ordination of women, although when we first talked it was, 'Oh, no, there's no problem'; but it clearly was a problem.

A further source of frustration was voiced by another interviewee who felt that insufficient notice was taken of information readily to hand:

[The DDO] had got College reports, so he could have had quite a good idea of my particular abilities,

> but it almost seems as if [these] are totally irrelevant;
> you're on the bottom rung, just a new deacon who's
> seen not to be able to do anything.

Apart from suggesting a low expectation of curates, this point is significant in that it appears to be unusual for training incumbents to know very much about ordinands before they come to look at the parish, or before offering the job. As noted earlier, bishops and DDOs have a lot of information from the selection and training processes, but it would appear that this is never disclosed, possibly on the grounds of confidentiality, even though it is essential for making a balanced decision about an appointment. It might be argued that as long as the bishop is satisfied that the person is suitable for ordination, this is enough; but that hardly helps a prospective training incumbent who will need to work with a curate day by day. This reflects an ignorance of basic interviewing practice and can lead to unfortunate, if not disastrous, appointments. Information is particularly important where curates have some expectation of being more than just a pair of hands:

> It's one thing having a task divided by labour where
> you simply do your bit; it's quite another thing working
> collaboratively so that all parts of the task are
> worked on by everyone: that to me is the difference
> between collaboration and dividing up labour.

Impressions of parishes before ordination are inevitably put to the test by actually having to work there. In view of the criticisms offered so far, it is important to stress that most interviewees were positive about the ministries they exercised. One enjoyed

> . . . working with people in this community . . . and
> unapologetically doing it because I'm a Christian
> . . . being involved in whatever's going on and trying
> to say that the gospel's got something to do with this.

Another appreciated

> . . . the overview aspect of it that takes on board
> not only people's lives but also the community in
> which they live and tries to make sense of the total
> package. I think in previous jobs one looked at
> small aspects of a person's life or community and I
> felt that's artificial because you can only look at the
> total person. So it's a sense of all that coming
> together and people being spiritual beings who for
> a while live on this planet.

The criticism and disappointments fell into two main areas. The
first was a sense of a lack of definition or clear responsibility.
One woman made a telling comparison with other work:

> Having been on maternity leave for four months, lots
> of people have said to me, 'Have they got someone
> in to do your job while you're not there?' and I've
> said it doesn't work like that; at which point they've
> said, 'Well, isn't your job worth anything?' because
> they've worked in jobs with a clear [purpose]. . . .
> It's not that I'm indispensable, but that I'm quite
> easily dispensable.

This was echoed by others:

> I have next to no responsibility; I'm the curate, which
> means that I don't have any clout in the place. I
> don't say I want power, but I can be dismissed in a
> way that is quite destructive. . . . Sometimes . . . I
> just wonder what the hell I'm here for. There's an
> intangibility to it which on a bad day I find quite
> depressing. . . . [I can just] wander up and down
> the road a bit, give people a stroke now and then
> and they purr a bit maybe.

Some people found that the role of curate was unnecessarily restricting:

> I find some of the committee meetings I go to, within the parish . . . a bit frustrating being in the role [of] assistant curate and sometimes having to think twice about what I want to say.

or sensed that they were being excluded:

> I wasn't allowed to be involved to the extent I wanted to be . . . and not being told what was happening.

As mentioned in Chapter 1 there is a long-standing belief in the Church of England that curates are either difficult or over-enthusiastic, and this may be used to counter these comments. But it is important to recognise that curates increasingly come from work in other occupations, some of which are very demanding and have called for a good deal of skill and expertise. It is short-sighted to overlook this and assume that the new curate is incapable of taking appropriate responsibilities.

Almost inevitably, there were difficulties in working with training incumbents, some of which give a clue to frustrations about lack of responsibility.

> When I arrived, the vicar . . . was a terribly nice chap but not necessarily very good as a trainer. On the first morning after I arrived we said Morning Prayer together and he said, 'See you tomorrow'! . . . and it sort of continued in that vein. . . . So, basically, I had to fairly quickly decide what I intended to do and how I was going to set about doing it; and do it for myself.

Again:

I found my vicar very hard to work with; I remember the first few weeks I was in the parish feeling very at sea because he was a very laid-back character who didn't give you any direction at all, and I wondered quite what I was supposed to be doing there. I had to actually sit down and set myself some objectives, what I wanted to achieve out of this period as a curate, or at least the first year, and once I'd done that and talked them over with somebody else I felt much happier about what I was supposed to be doing.

There were other issues for some people, however:

... it's a very obviously hierarchical structure; a lot of the things I get asked to do or not to do aren't because of the way I'm doing things but because he wants to assert his authority and power over me ... but he'll never say that.

and:

The first year kind of whizzes past and you don't know whether you're coming or going and you *know* that you don't know what's happening: then in the second and third year . . . the problem is that you *know* you could be doing it better than the person who's running it, and it's when that realisation takes effect that utter frustration sets in, especially when any suggestion you make is taken as a personal affront or criticism; you're just paralysed into not doing anything. The only things you're allowed to do are what you know [the vicar] doesn't want to do.

It may be that the lack of responsibility for some curates is less a matter of ignoring their abilities, more that training incumbents are too preoccupied with their own work to help their curates think about what they are doing. This may be reinforced by the all-too-frequently reactive nature of ministry for many clergy. If the work is primarily about responding to emergencies and unanticipated events, newcomers will initially have little to do until they have these demands made upon them. But training requires a systematic introduction to work, and this clearly did not happen for many of the curates.

For others there were questions about what the church was about:

> I found parish life very inward-looking, really; it's very easy if you're not careful to get sucked into the round of doing the things the church does and just maintaining the church. . . . It was a big parish; it had a population of about 14,000, so the pressure of occasional offices, three or four funerals a week, lots of baptisms and weddings, meant that you could very easily just get sucked into doing that, doing Sunday services and doing all the administration . . .

The public aspects of ministry might be of doubtful value sometimes:

> There are some things you have to do because you're the clergy . . . and that's got a very positive place . . . but sometimes I think that 'showing the flag' is really a bit of a waste of time.

as well as the staff group itself:

> When things work well in a team it's a very positive thing; when things don't work so well it's quite a drawback . . . as soon as a member leaves the

positions change and I've seen that work positively, [though] also negatively; a cause of frustration.

While sometimes it was a struggle to

. . . [prevent] my horizons collapsing round me under trivia . . . not trivia, but things that prevent me doing what I'm there to do.

There will always be a gap between the expectations people have of a job, or a place, or a colleague, and of living and working with the reality. Anglican curates are not the only people to have to face a measure of disillusionment when starting a new job and be faced with the need for readjustments of expectations which this causes. What is significant about the people interviewed here is that they have often had to abandon reasonable expectations because the structure in which they are working cannot address the genuine need for these to be fulfilled. However much initial responsibility is laid at training incumbents' doors, in the end a greater responsibility rests with those who devise and perpetuate the present system of appointments. As one curate commented of a training incumbent with whom they had experienced considerable difficulties over several years:

To be fair, I really think it's not the guy's fault; he just wasn't trained how to be a training incumbent. In about three or four curates' time, he'll make a very good training incumbent, it's just no one told him what he was supposed to be doing. . . . No idea about teaching techniques, or adult education, or management skills or groupwork, because when he was trained you never did [any] . . . so considering the guy was doing it blind without any support or encouragement from anybody, he probably did a very good job.

NOTES

1 For more on this, see my article 'Clergy Careers in the Church of England this Century' in *Crucible*, July-September 1995, pp. 127-136.

2 It is important to recognise that Methodist ministers are not ordained before they first take charge in a circuit; in the intervening period they are laypeople, but with a dispensation from Conference to administer the sacraments and they are allowed to wear clerical dress.

CHAPTER 3

Work: the expectation and the reality

My bottom point was . . . when we had to walk from the church hall . . . to the church through a dark car park full of potholes full of water. We lost several old ladies down these potholes but I couldn't get anyone to recognise that this was a problem so I decided I would have to do something about it. Another church car park has too much gravel in it so every time I went there . . . I would fill up a plastic container with gravel and fill a hole. Eventually, five weeks later, somebody noticed the holes were being filled up with gravel and that I was doing it: at which point I thought, 'What am I doing here?' – but they're now thinking of doing something about the car park.

'HE ONLY WORKS ONE DAY A WEEK'

Discussing the work done by ministers of religion often turns on questions of definition. The most obvious of these is whether a distinction can be made between what clergy do and what might be done by any Christian. The jibe about only working one day a week reflects the reality that conducting public worship can be the only work done by ministers which is seen by many members of a church congregation, much less by the public who often see nothing of them from one month to another. Even if public worship is extended beyond Sundays to encompass weekday services and rites of passage such as weddings and funerals, there still seems to be relatively little to occupy ministers' time while others are earning a living in factories, shops and offices. Going to visit a housebound elderly person or the mother and toddler group in the church hall, particularly where such a visit has no overtly religious activity such as prayer, and includes social chat and a cup of tea, does not look to many people like work; at most it might be part of an expression of neighbourly concern. Similarly, church committees and educational activities are for most people voluntary involvements outside of paid work time, or something taken up when a lifetime of paid employment has ended with retirement. All this applies with more force in the case of social activities; by definition these are leisure activities undertaken for mutual enjoyment.

In recent decades this ambiguity over ministers' work has been compounded by the emergence of an increasing number of voluntary lay and ordained ministers in the Church of England. The office of Reader has existed for well over a century, but it has taken on new significance in recent years with the continuing decline in numbers of full-time paid clergy, notably in rural areas. This decline has also encouraged the recruitment and ordination of non-stipendiary ministers who, like Readers, are emerging into greater prominence with the decline in the stipendiary ministry and can now be licensed by bishops as incumbents of parishes rather than being consigned to everlasting curacies. A third factor has been the increasing relaxation of the belief that everything of any significance which happens in a parish church has to be done or directed by clergy. Lay people now undertake a great many roles which, even a quarter of a century ago, would have been seen as clerical preserves. Liturgical activities such as reading the scriptures, leading intercessions, directing music, preaching, helping administer communion and, in some places, assisting in ritual laying hands on the sick are perhaps the most prominent, but other roles, such as teaching adults and children, leading and convening prayer and study groups, offering pastoral care, counselling, and caring for buildings are often undertaken primarily by lay church members. Some are officially endorsed by a bishop's licence or the church council's mandate, but others are involved simply because they are there and willing to be so. The rise of other forms of ministry has been significant because so many of the inherited ideas which clergy have about their work have been influenced by their concept of themselves as professional people with a claim to an exclusive expertise and monopoly of the right to practise it. Anthony Russell has discussed[1] how the clergy have often failed to have as clearly defined a practice of professionalism as found elsewhere, unlike doctors and lawyers; but, whatever the hard realities, the ideal of professionalism was often presumed and it is this which the broadening of ministry has undermined.

One way out of this ambiguity might be for clergy to remodel their ideas about ministry along the lines of bodies like charities, where much of the work is done by volunteers but where small paid staffs exist in order to service the organisation and work alongside the volunteers, equipping them to be more effective in what they choose to do in their spare time. This model seems to have much to commend it, but it can also throw into sharp focus the clergy's lack of some of the areas of particular expertise, such as financial or personal management, education, groupwork or counselling skills, which charities' paid staffs may be required to have. Moreover, clergy often have an ambiguous view of themselves as professionals, as will be discussed below, and although some do possess considerable skills which are accredited by other practitioners outside of the churches, this is neither generally so, nor is it required of them; a point which reinforces some observations in Chapter 2 about the selection of training incumbents.

Indeed, to many clergy ministry may not be about having a particular clutch of professional skills and qualifications; it is about living out the Gospel in the world, showing the love of God in Christ to others and 'keeping the rumour of God alive'. This view is reflected in the oft-quoted belief that clergy are not paid a salary, as other workers are; instead, the stipend is a payment to free them from the need to earn a living and thereby to allow them to concentrate on the work to which God has called them. Just as they receive a 'non-wage', so their work is a 'non-job'. Thus everyday calculations about hours and conditions of work, remuneration, contract and liability are side-stepped in the name of vocation. The strength of this image undoubtedly lies in the sense of 'otherness' which vocation to ministry claims, and through this a strong implicit critique of everyday values and assumptions.

Conversely, its weakness seems to lie in the difficulty of giving that critique any tangible reality. What can, and arguably often does, happen is that ministry becomes both heavily reactive, always responding to external demands or pressures; and also tends to pursue a strong implicit agenda, often focused on ecclesiastical concerns. The reality of the clergy's situation is that they are not just free spirits, liberated to move through the world and engage with its life as God moves them; they are employees of a large and long-established human institution with a great many institutional procedures, assumptions, codes of conduct, buildings, money and other resources. The Church of England is historically also a great corporation of state, linked in all sorts of ways to the life of the people locally, regionally and nationally, and the focus of extensive expectations, even from those who are not counted among its members.

A further reality is that the formative Christian documents of the New Testament do not presuppose a special, ordained, theologically defined professional ministry at all. Jesus is depicted in the gospels as choosing disciples, some of whom form a particular group around him and eventually become known as apostles. But they co-exist with other groups, not least groups of women, and after Jesus' death there are problems about how this group is to be maintained, who may call themselves an apostle – a particular and personal concern of the ex-Pharisee Saul of Tarsus – and whether they have any continuing function within the Christian *diaspora*. The gospel-writers not only depict the disciples in different ways – Mark, in particular, seeing them as frequently ignorant, self-interested and obtuse – but also tend to use them in their stories as a foil for Jesus' teaching, or an audience for his particular sayings. Apart from being with him and sharing the privations of his itinerant ministry, they have no clear functions; sometimes they help control the crowds, or help in preaching or exorcisms, or go ahead of the main party to alert people of its arrival.

Part of the background to these images of discipleship may be Jesus' belief that the End of the Age was imminent and therefore all human institutions, even those hallowed by the Law and the Prophets, were purely a short-term reality. The difficulty this has created for the churches is how to translate a loose, ill-defined and changing set of images of discipleship into a pattern for a formally constituted, historic ministry. The Church of England has a further problem inasmuch as there is no detailed central agreement about either the nature or practice of ordained ministry; this handicaps the process of devising a generally accepted training process for ministers after ordination. Training before ordination is organised around the answers which training agencies provide to ABM in response to two questions: 'What ordained ministry does the Church of England require?' and 'What is the shape of the educational programme best suited for equipping people to exercise this ministry?'[2] This inevitably reflects the plurality of ideas contained within the Church of England, though with the proviso that ABM, on behalf of the bishops, sets the parameters of acceptability for the process as a whole. There is no parallel process for POT. The particular consequence is that all the responsibility for inducting newly ordained ministers into their daily work is frequently put into the hands of the training incumbent, who, as we shall see, is all too often unwilling or unable to carry this out.

THE CURATES' WORK SURVEY

Allowing for the problems of definition outlined above, curates and other ministers find plenty to occupy their time. In order to find out more about the kinds of work they undertook, the interviewees were asked to complete a time-use survey, the results of which were then tabulated to see how they divided their time between different areas of work. The more detailed results of the survey are given in Appendix 2, but a summary is offered here to indicate the main characteristics of the curates' work.

The time-use survey was intended to be as comprehensive as possible and included 39 possible categories of work, though respondents were allowed to indicate other categories of their own, as a few did. In order to make the results as balanced as possible, each interviewee was asked to choose any two consecutive weeks between January and May which might be expected to be typical of their regular work, but excluding planned special occasions like Ash Wednesday, Holy Week, stewardship campaigns, or absences for holidays. They were asked to indicate the time spent on each activity to the nearest half-hour, including travelling time to and from it. This inevitably offers an impressionistic account rather than a precise study, but it will be adequate for our purposes.

One of the most obvious points to emerge from the survey is the fragmented nature of ministry, embracing a large number of activities often pursued for a very limited period of time. Twenty-eight of the recorded categories took up an hour and a half or less per week and only the conduct of regular public worship took more than five hours a week. Moreover, these are total figures and some activities were undertaken in blocks of an hour or less at a time. Some interviewees commented that the variety of work was one of its attractions, but continually starting and stopping tasks must impose limits on any person's ability to function effectively and may in time erode job satisfaction.

There was also some indication that as people progress through ministry from ordination there is a tendency to cover a narrower spread of activities, but to undertake more regularly the ones which are done, offering a more consistent working week; this was particularly the case with those respondents who had become incumbents. Even so, most people's ministries remain very fragmented.

Despite the apparently bewildering assortment of activities, it was possible to group them under main headings and these are described in table 3:1 below.

TABLE 3:1. GENERAL CATEGORIES OF MINISTERIAL WORK

Category	most/least hours per week	average hours per week
Leader of Public Worship/Preacher	20/9.5	14
Pastor	19/9.5	13
Work with adults	5.5/1	3
Work with children	4.5/1	3
Organiser	15/8	11
Representative of the Church	11/2	5
Personal development	11.5/7.5	9
Total hours per week	68.5/54	58

Three main activities, Leader of Public Worship, Pastor and Organiser, are evident and account for an average of 38 out of 58 hours a week, or 65 per cent of work time recorded here. Although this is a very small sample, and therefore not able to support too many conclusions, it is significant that neither work with groups of children or adults, nor the representative role is very strongly emphasised.

It is also clear that the working week, averaging 58 hours, was a long one, but the convention that clergy have one day off a week means that this was spread over six days, averaging ten hours a day. However, closer examination suggests that the curates were working to a more varied pattern. Each week, one day between Monday and Friday was a day off and the other four were 'long days' starting around 8 am, often with some act of worship, and ending any time between 9 and 11 pm with only one-hour breaks for lunch and an evening meal. Weekends were two 'short days', work being concentrated around certain activities, which on Saturdays included weddings, social events or some urgent piece of work from earlier in the week; on Sundays work focused on morning and evening public worship. Apart from these specific tasks, no other work was done and opportunity was taken to spend time with friends or families, do household tasks, or take some relaxation. Work and leisure were governed by the availability of other people; hence the need to work during evenings, but also to find some time for shared leisure, a reality particularly for married people with children, but affecting all respondents. Chapter 5 will show how the curates felt these pressures affected their social lives, but suffice it to say here that a number of difficulties were apparent, particularly when it was wished to meet people beyond the immediate family circle.

CURATES' REFLECTIONS ON STARTING WORK

How did the curates react to starting work in this environment? They were asked a number of interrelated questions to elicit their reflections, which, it must be remembered, were anything from one to five years after the event. Initially they were asked whether there were any memories which particularly stuck in their minds of the earliest days after ordination. They were then asked whether they could recall instances which brought home to them that other people regarded them as ministers, and whether they could recall instances which made them see themselves in that way. Two more questions explored the opposite range of feelings, the first being to ask what experiences, past or present, made them doubt themselves as ministers. To test the strength of these doubts they were asked whether they had ever felt they made a mistake by being ordained, whatever their present feelings.

Since ordination confers the right to wear clerical dress, it is not altogether surprising that a number of the curates should comment on this as an abiding memory of their earliest days in ministry. The clerical collar might make people self-conscious:

> It took me a while to get used to wearing a dog-collar; I remember walking down the road smiling at everybody – I just thought I had to! . . . I'm identified with the church. . . . That's still there, actually . . . people talk to me differently than if I haven't got it on.

Women had been eligible to be ordained deacon from 1986, but Anglican women clergy were still something of a novelty, as one recalled:

> I felt very public . . . when I got onto a bus . . . the driver looked me up and down – I think I had a short skirt on – and said, 'You aren't really one of them lady vicars, are you?' and I said, 'Well, I am really!'

Sometimes the clerical collar opened up the possibility of unexpected theological discussions:

> I was walking down the street in my dog-collar – it must have been the day after I was ordained – and a man came up to me and said, 'Can I talk to you about something, Father? . . . Will my dog go to heaven when it dies?'

For others there was an unwelcome aspect to this:

> There's a clerical persona and I never felt I wanted
> to put that on, but it's thrust upon you . . . both
> within the Church and outside it. If you go round
> wearing a dog-collar people treat you in a different
> way . . . and I actually hate that; I want to be
> treated as a human being . . . there are all sorts of
> little things; people don't swear in your presence,
> or they'll apologise if they swear at you and treat
> you with deference. Certainly within the Church
> there's an awful lot of myth about the clergy: who
> they are, how they're different and better than
> everyone else. I find it very hard to live up to that
> expectation.

Another very public consequence of ordination are the tasks
associated with the conduct of public worship. One person
recalled:

> Preparing for my first toddlers' service . . . I found
> I had to get into tune with it . . . I had difficulty
> learning the songs and the verses and rhymes they
> knew. . . . [Now] even the under-fives know there's
> a liturgical difference between the vicar and me!

For others, conducting funerals was a testing process:

> Coping with [people's] expectations in a way that
> was sensitive and also realistic I found particularly
> difficult. . . . I had to do a funeral visit very soon
> after I was ordained, of a child who had been mur-
> dered . . . and clearly the mother was looking to
> me for reassurance about something, she didn't
> know what and I didn't know what, actually. I'd
> never encountered that sort of situation before. . . .

At that point I realised that I was expected to say something that would comfort her in a way which the efficiency of the undertakers couldn't and the apparent indifference of her family wouldn't.

Another recalled having only taken part in one funeral when

> . . . next week a funeral came in and [the incumbent] said, 'It's so-and-so, at the crem at - - -; I've never been there myself but you'll find a clergy stall and a button to push. I think [the crematorium] is off a roundabout on the bypass.' I was angry about that, not just for myself . . . but . . . [because of] wanting to do my best for these people over the loss of a relatively young man, I think, and being fobbed off by such an ill-prepared approach to it.

With ordination came a new place of work which had to be explored and understood:

> I spent the first couple of months walking the parish and mapping the parish . . . and that made me feel in some ways at home and comfortable. I've never had the opportunity to do it since, but I'm really glad I took the opportunity then; I know the parish in a way my colleagues have chosen not to. Because I was to be a parish resource I felt the need to get engaged with that.

There was also a new home, though the fact that this was church property could be a mixed blessing:

> One of the things I had to come to terms with in the first six months was . . . the lack of privacy, although . . . I could close the door and I don't have many callers at the house; but the phone used

to go at awkward times, and the feeling of readjust-
ment was quite acute; also, coming from a residential
college to the life of a single woman again . . . which
was quite difficult. [There was also] the feeling that
although this was my home . . . somehow it was
open to other people. . . . People would come . . .
[and say], 'Oh, you've done this to the house since
- - - left'; I felt, 'It's mine now, it's none of your
business what I've done to it.'

Several people recalled the sense that they were not much
welcomed by the congregation, or their new colleagues:

I remember feeling . . . that they didn't actually
want me. There was a mission on when I got here.
. . . They'd done nothing whatever to this house
except repair a bit of woodworm . . . and upstairs
it's in fairly bad decorative order. Nobody invited
me to a meal, or indeed even to coffee . . . all the
approaches that were made I had to make myself.
People . . . were busy with their mission. I felt very
lonely and very out on a limb. . . . I felt quite hurt
and thought, 'Gosh, I don't know how I'm going
to cope with this.'

while another said:

I remember going to the incumbent's house and
really not being received. If I was a training incumbent with a newly ordained curate there would be
certain things I would expect to have already prepared; a map of the parish with the parish boundaries, a list of the people, a plan of duties, a
discussion of what we would do together in the
initial stages and a general talk about hopes and
expectations and areas of weakness and strength

where I'd want to develop. There was none of
that. . . . We chatted for a bit . . . we did two visits
together and then he said, 'Do your own thing.' I
just felt that was not enough; I felt cast out, almost
– with this terrible restriction: [he told me that
there were] certain people I was not allowed to go
and see.

People's attitudes to women's ordination could provoke difficulties:

The period when I was ordained deacon was the
time of the vote [on women's ordination as priests]
and a lay reader had attached herself to the church
. . . [who] turned out to be very anti the ordination
of women; so my first six to seven months was a
time of survival; that was very tough. . . . No one
told me that this had happened, so when I arrived
I was met by this other person who gave the
impression she had been there a long time . . . so it
was all very difficult.

The disparate and unstructured timetable caused difficulties
for several of the curates:

There was the newness of everything, so many new
experiences, that . . . whenever I had some spare time
I was running through my head what I had to do
next . . . It wasn't that I had nothing to do; it was that
I hadn't learned which things had to be done now,
which things had to be done tomorrow, which things
had to be done next week; which things couldn't
be done today and had to be left to next week. All
that newness did create loads of anxieties . . .

Colleagues might not be very helpful, either:

Should I be working all the time? I knew I shouldn't
. . . I remember going for a drink with the vicar's
son . . . When he turned up he said, 'When I told
my dad I was going for a drink with you tonight,
my dad said, "It's not her day off, is it?"' That just
confirmed those feelings that I ought to be on the
go all the time – that's the impression he gave.
When I tried telling him . . . he said, 'Do you find
yourself watching telly all the afternoon? . . . I had
[that] problem: I used to watch telly all day': but I
thought, 'That's *not* my problem!'

Another observed:

On the one hand I was held back from doing things
because I'm not experienced enough . . . on the
other hand [the vicar] will throw me into things
when it's convenient. . . . Especially as a deacon . . .
there I was, cassock and dog-collar, and all I was
allowed to do [in the liturgy] was read the gospel –
wow! . . . and on the other hand being dropped
into things that were too heavy to have to be doing
in the first few weeks.

There might also be contrasts with earlier careers:

I'd been used to a job where I was in charge of a
department; I could make decisions . . . suddenly,
despite all the warnings of college, to be completely
de-skilled [and to be told,] 'Well, actually it's nothing to do with you, is it?'; that was hard . . . It
was harder than I'd thought, to be treated like
a fourteen-year-old: not by the incumbent [but]
you were almost like the pet dog sometimes; 'Oh,
they get younger, don't they?'; 'You don't look old
enough'.

For others, these anxieties disappeared when they found themselves in a position of responsibility. One curate told how, a few weeks after they had been ordained deacon, their incumbent had gone on holiday:

> I remember thinking, 'How am I going to cope? I've got this parish and I can't even think how to do simple things!' But then after he'd been gone a week I thought, 'Don't hurry back!'

Because working in parish ministry is a public role, it is important for clergy to sense that other people recognise them as such. In the early months this is particularly important in helping them to get used to the role and be able to develop and adapt it to themselves. But there needs also to be a parallel process by which the curate begins to recognise that they really are a minister and feel some integrity in that role. The two questions exploring these interrelated experiences revealed a range of events and feelings. To some it was a particular occasion that revealed other people's recognition of their ministry, significantly often connected with death or bereavement:

> [One day] filling up my car with petrol, a chap came over to me – I'd got my collar on – he said, 'I know this isn't terribly appropriate, but do you have two seconds? I'm a Catholic and my priest doesn't seem to want to listen to me at all; my daughter died last night, she was only eighteen.'

Another recalled the aftermath of a road accident:

> This was something which was very important for me . . . the family all live round about here; there was something about turning up on the doorsteps of these people the day after, not really knowing any

of them . . . and their response to me, which was partly anger and partly . . . relief . . . they felt I should be there but they were angry I was there because it shouldn't have happened anyway, these people shouldn't have died in a car accident. . . . I don't know how I was able to help, but I must have done because they almost feel I'm like one of the family now; quite strange. But I think it had to do with the fact that it was more than just me turning up . . . you're not sure why you're there, but I felt I had to be there: and talking about . . . God at all, and God's love and whatever that means in this situation, was difficult. I didn't actually say anything, really, just turned up and said, 'I've seen you around, heard what's happened and felt I had to come round.'

For another, the process was more gradual:

Initially I was thought of as 'the boy' . . . and compared to some of the clergy in the deanery I was the boy! . . . identifying that [I had a capacity for] working with people who were terminally ill . . . [led to others] seeing me differently; I wasn't the boy who was laughing and joking all the time, I was somebody else.

Sometimes the sense of other people's recognition was more general, as in these two instances:

People saw that you represented something and most people seemed to think it was worthwhile, even if some of them had little acquaintance with it.

There's 'We want to get to know you'; and some people desperately want to get to know you and be known by me. . . . It wasn't people coming out with their deepest confessions to me straight away; it's not that sort of place.

Another person mentioned a rather more complex attitude of other people towards him:

> You realise that, in the eyes of someone else, you are sexually attractive . . . I guess they kind of fancy the role . . . it may be that being a priest, wearing clerical robes, will somehow be a safety barrier; they won't be hurt, they won't be abused . . . they feel protected because they know I won't treat them in ways that other people have treated them. . . . That . . . naive confidence actually takes something away from me as a sexual human being.

In response to the parallel question about how they came to recognise themselves as ministers, a number of curates cited occasions when they had been given responsibilities, particularly liturgical ones:

> [As a deacon] when the vicar was away I would take the whole Sunday morning eucharist from the reserved sacrament; the first time I did that I felt, 'That has such a different feel to it; I'm the one who does this on behalf [of the congregation]' – quite a priestly feeling.

> After the first few months I was put in charge of all baptisms . . . whether it was slightly type-casting a woman to do baptisms I'm not sure. It's also got something to do with the vicar's time management on a Sunday afternoon. It had the effect of giving you a role, which is fine, in that I've done all the bread-and-butter ones in this area. It caused friction later

on in that [the vicar] would choose to do all the
ones that were 'high profile'.

Others mentioned more general and gradual realisations,
often prompted by the reactions of others:

It was partly being identified with this bunch 'the
clergy'; there were conversations which almost went
down the line of 'them and us', from people in the
congregation . . . it dawned on me after a while
that actually they meant me! . . . I was one of 'them'.

We went on holiday . . . we'd been down there last
year and nobody asked me what my job was. This
year [when we went to church] the vicar asked and
when I told him he said, 'Oh, I'd have polished up
the sermon a bit if I'd known.'

One person put it in more explicitly theological terms:

I think it's to do with being something wider than
just here; with the catholicity of the Church; to do
with . . . being called to do this . . . something which
it's right to be doing . . . with my vision of what the
gospel's all about . . . feeling like . . . a *provocateur*
of the Gospel. It's got something to do with urgency
and the way I feel I live out my Christian life. . . .
It's got something to do with personal feelings and
[also] something to do with . . . representing more
than just me.

Turning these questions around invited the curates to consider
what made them doubt themselves as ministers. For a number,
this focused on perceptions of doing their work badly:

I sometimes go through phases where I think, 'If I
suddenly disappeared, they wouldn't notice', which

is not really self-pity. But then suddenly I get pulled up short and I realise how important I am in their lives . . . the fact that I've bothered to go round and see somebody, whereas I think I've just gone and had a cup of tea and a biscuit.

Others were troubled by a lack of tangible results:

Recently . . . I was looking two years on and asked, 'What, as a result of my being here, has changed in this parish? . . . [among other issues] has any of all this funeral work resulted in anyone becoming members of the church?' and as far as I can see, no. . . . It's obviously not that simple, but to many people the result of me being here doesn't seem to have changed anything; I may have maintained it, or there may have been other kinds of change, but you have to enquire more deeply to identify these. . . . I've kept objectives for myself, but they're the kind of service-type objectives like to run a confirmation course . . . so I felt uneasy about whether I could actually assess whether I've made a difference or not.

Again:

One thing which is undermining is that the identity of the job is so nebulous. . . . Even if I know what I'm doing, [most of] the rest of the 15,000 people in the parish don't.

Colleagues' attitudes and expectations, spoken or unspoken, clearly affected how people felt they were coping, as one person recalled:

You start off . . . and you work alongside colleagues, [the vicar] in particular, who are absolutely on top of it and you realise he's cramming in twice as much as you are. . . . Things like funerals are very, very draining. [The vicar's] wife was very sympathetic about that; she said to him, 'Well, don't you remember when first you did a funeral you were absolutely exhausted, you used to collapse in a heap?' He'd forgotten that.

Laypeople's expectations might be similarly discouraging:

When people put upon you that image of being the all-knowing dispenser of wisdom and spiritual insight, holiness and blessing, and all the rest of it, you think, 'Whatever do they think about me?' . . . because actually I'm no different to them in terms of being a human being and I don't want to be.

Or:

I'm very jealous about my private space and ordained ministry is a very public occupation. I find it very difficult to suppress feelings of irritation when the phone rings and someone on the other end really needn't have phoned me, especially around tea-time or [the children's] bathtime. . . . The feelings [I have] I regard as unworthy for someone in the position I am. . . . It doesn't get easier; if anything, I find it gets more difficult.

For some people, events occasionally brought home feelings of neglecting their talents, or being unable to respond appropriately . . .

Sometimes going from one extreme to another in a series of visits is hard going and then you sound like a gibbering idiot; you can't make any sense at all. . . . People ask you deep theological questions and you can't find the equipment at that moment to talk to them on the level they want you to because you've been wittering on about leg ulcers previously. . . . [Once] someone wanted to get to grips with the nature of the Church and ministry and where God fitted into all this and I was struggling . . . had I come straight out of college I'd have given him a run for his money but . . . [there had been] years of those skills and thought-patterns not being used.

. . . or simply becoming mechanical:

> The doubts come with . . . 'Have you actually prayed enough?' – you suddenly realise, 'Have you actually prayed?' You think, 'Good grief, you've said all the words, but have you actually done it?' . . . After priesting, you're about half-way through the third service and you think, 'I've said all these words, but have I been actually there? . . . what right have I to stand there?'

For some people ministry challenged long-established assumptions and self-expectations . . .

> I don't like being wrong, I never have done; and I made myself a success in my previous career by being right; you had to be right. So there's something inherent in me that doesn't like being wrong.

. . . or the lack of helpful comparisons:

> I get disillusioned; at the end of the day I know that it won't make much difference when I leave the place . . . [other clergy] who are remembered

very well are probably not doing the kind of job I'd want to be remembered for doing. It's about not setting too much store by what you do.

There was also a recognition of the need to live with doubts . . .

However many years it's been, and it's now been eleven since I felt positively called by God, it still seems a surprise. I don't think I will ever be so convinced that I'm meant to be a priest that I will have the confidence of the fundamentalist.

. . . though the Church's theology could be a problem too:

It's all this stuff the Church throws out about, 'You're a sinner, you're unworthy' . . . while at the same time chucking out the message that you're the beloved, the chosen; it's mixed messages, it hasn't got its act together about what we are. More and more I want to go down the path of being cared for and being part of the sons and daughters of God, and not having to beat my breast and say how awful I am.

Did people ever think they had made a mistake by being ordained? A significant number of people clearly had thought this at some time, even if they did not think so all the time. For many it was not so much a matter of doubting their calling as doubting the validity of the Church's expectations of them. One person encountered this doubt very early:

During the first summer . . . I couldn't grab hold of what being ordained [was]. What had been a leisure pursuit, almost . . . suddenly is everything; you go to church every day . . . a major part of your life is talking about churchy things, or if it's not, it's at a pathetically shallow level. . . . When you get buckets of that, you think, 'Why did I do this?'

A woman replied:

> No: but had I not been ordained priest I might have [thought so]. . . . What has kept me going all through training has been . . . that I feel relatively objectively that the talents or gifts that I have are ideally suited to the job of a parish priest. . . . A lot of the arguments against the ordination of women were that they wouldn't be able to manage it. . . . [Not being ordained priest] would have meant that I spent my life as a curate . . . I would have felt blocked.

Another person was helped by people's responses to him:

> Sometimes I think the Church may have made a mistake: I'm not strictly orthodox; not what they usually expect by a clergyman. But it's something that people have warmed to, I think.

Conversely, several people found their perception of the Church's expectations were particularly burdensome:

> Churchy things really quite irritate me . . . this false piety . . . pigeon-holing things into 'church' and 'non-church' . . . of not being allowed to speak of profound things in ordinary life because you're being 'religious' . . . [church buildings are often] extraordinarily sterile and that doesn't speak to me of God's involvement with the world, or the Incarnation. . . . I recognise myself as a 'margins' person . . . [but] if you're a maverick, you never know whether you're going to be kicked out or distrusted by those in authority.

Another observed:

> I think the whole thing about professional ministry
> is vastly overdone . . . I often fail to live up to people's
> expectations of what a minister is or should be; I
> know that and they don't, most of the time. . . . It
> bothers me that they have these unrealistic expec-
> tations and therefore I feel as if I don't fit some-
> how . . . I have some very irreverent views about
> the church; I don't have a very high doctrine of the
> Church, or of priesthood and I have all sorts of
> doubts about God; and the way that I live and we
> live as a family doesn't always fit in with people's
> image of what ministerial life is like. . . . I'm not
> sure I share all the Church's self-perception of
> what it's about . . . There's this kind of unwritten
> assumption that floats around the Church that
> everybody needs [it] and that everybody really
> ought to be in church, and it structures the way to
> God and all that that implies – it's the way to hap-
> piness and wholeness and all the rest of it. Actually
> I'm continually amazed at the amount of bad feeling
> and bad relationships that there are in the Church
> and I think that people are much better off without
> it, really.

For some the matter was more about personal integrity . . .

> I often feel that I could live more honestly . . . as a
> human being if I wasn't ordained. . . . It's a lot to
> do with [other people's] expectations . . . and I
> think it was a big mistake from my family's point
> of view.

. . . or practical usefulness:

I do sometimes feel, 'Could I serve humanity better if I was still [doing my former job]? . . . would I not be a Christian alongside other Christians without wearing a dog-collar and all the rest of it?' . . . all of the job could be done by someone who wasn't ordained, in my opinion including breaking the bread and sharing the cup . . . but I suppose it is good that there are those of us who are doing this full-time. I sometimes think it's a question of a model of ministry that I have . . . when I first started thinking of ordained ministry I was thinking of non-stipendiary ministry and I suppose in the back of my mind I wonder if I hold more to that than to stipendiary ministry. . . . I'm not sure where this will take me in the future.

Another recalled feeling trapped by circumstances:

I don't think it was acknowledged how insecure [training] is; giving up a career in which I was doing well, no property, because we'd sold our house . . . and no prospect of getting back to that because I'd changed. . . . Suddenly I felt very insecure but I couldn't go back to being the person I was before . . . what on earth would I do? I wasn't qualified to do anything: and I guess those insecurities were burning away at me when I came into a parish which didn't actually over-affirm my ministry and vocation. . . . If I didn't have a strong sense of vocation and knew God wanted me to be a priest I'd never have got through college and I certainly would never have finished my curacy.

For one person, living with a sense of having possibly been mistaken was an integral part of life:

I've thought many times that I made a mistake being

ordained, but I've always come back to the conviction that this is what God has called me to do: I've never lost that conviction . . . a strange restlessness within oneself that there is a point in all this, there is work to be done and a particular work to be done at a particular time: I still hold on to that conviction and it comes to me from time to time, unexpectedly.

NOTES

1 Anthony Russell, *The Clerical Profession*, London, SPCK (1980).

2 *Education for the Church's Ministry: the report of the Working Party on Assessment*, ACCM. Occasional Paper No. 22 (January 1987), p. 23f.

CHAPTER 4

Working together?
Colleagues and training

Sometimes it's a great joy; sometimes when I cele-
brate the Eucharist I feel this is a great privilege
and that's something which the Church has given
to me which I value greatly. At other times I feel
very bitter about the Church; I feel as if it expects
you to lose a lot of yourself to fit in with it. . . . [My
continued association with it is sustained by]
habit, the fact that it provides me with a living –
that's being very cynical! – [also] my belief in God
and I hope the Church expresses something of
that – I don't think it does it very well, but I don't
expect any human institutions to work very well,
that's just realistic. . . . I think if the Church were
honest about itself it would be much easier to live
with, but it has this very idealistic view of itself.

Enough has been said thus far to underline the key role training
incumbents are expected to play in curates' introduction to the
work of ministry. This role is officially recognised in dioceses
and the training programmes they devise for curates; and is the
reason why training incumbents are, in theory at least, carefully
selected. I hope it has also become clear from the observations
of the curates in this survey that most felt their relationship
with training incumbents to have been unsatisfactory on a
number of counts. As a broad generalisation, most interviewees
believed they had received considerably less help and support
from their incumbents than they had expected, while several
felt their colleagues had been hostile or excessively critical.

71

This is all the more worrying because almost all the incumbents had previously worked with at least one curate prior to the person I interviewed, so inexperience on their part seems an unlikely explanation. Conversely, it was clear that many curates had mixed feelings about this lack of active involvement, as expressed in one comment:

> The only positive thing . . . is that he isn't always asking me what I'm doing and . . . when I consult with my [contemporaries] that's fairly good. . . . He's never said, 'How do you spend your day?' I sometimes think he ought to be more concerned in an interested way; I sometimes tell him I've got things on and he never, ever asks, 'How did it go?' and I feel let down. . . . But he doesn't say, 'You shouldn't be involved in that.'

Most dioceses lay down minimal expectations of training incumbents' responsibilities towards their curates. These usually include a regular time each day for some act of worship, most likely the saying of Morning and Evening Prayer together; a weekly 'staff meeting' where the work of the forthcoming week can be planned; and some regular process of review and evaluation of the curate's work. At intervals during the curacy, the bishop will ask for reports on the curate's progress. One such is generally necessary at the end of the curate's first year, when they are preparing for ordination as a priest, and another at the end of the three-year Post-Ordination Training period, in preparation for the next job the curate may be offered. In recent years the practice of getting training incumbents and curates to draw up a 'working contract' for the year ahead has gained currency; these contracts are often arranged around a standard format approved by the director of POT and signed by them, the incumbent and curate, and possibly the bishop. Their purpose is to formalise the intention to work together and for the various parties to undertake some planning of the curate's time. Unfortunately, there seems a good deal of anecdotal evidence to suggest that, once drawn up, these contracts are either filed away and forgotten, or else incumbents make it clear that, while they have outwardly complied with diocesan expectations, they have no intention of doing what they have undertaken. Both these options are made possible by non-enforcement of the contract by diocesan staff, who may be unwilling to challenge incumbents' excuses for failing to observe it.

In many ways the term 'contract' is a misnomer; not only because, unlike other contracts, it is never enforced, but also because no attempt is made to establish clearly how it is to be put into effect. Mention has already been made of the frequently exhortatory tone of the training manuals which dioceses produce for incumbents and curates. There are frequently good ideas, suggestions for working together, helpful ways of thinking and planning, and encouragement of good practice. But there is rarely any stipulation of how much time any of this is to take; or some clear statement that incumbents and curates are to plan to make the time needed available in their working days. The frequently reactive and unstructured nature of much of the work done by clergy makes this difficult, because it challenges the culture of ministry to plan one's time and decline to be deflected by unexpected events. Saying 'no' is hard because it is assumed to indicate lack of selfless caring. Unfortunately, curates' comments reveal there was little sense that they might be entitled to expect at least some such attention; or that incumbents recognised that training a colleague and developing a good working relationship might more than repay the time and trouble devoted to it.

A cultural aversion to planning is one problem for training incumbents, but there is sometimes a feeling that in the past training incumbents were too directive and rigid in their expectations of curates, too inclined to stamp their own character and ways of working onto their junior colleagues. There is some truth in this; many clergy in the past were identifiable as 'Canon X's curates' because of the ways they conducted worship, or went about pastoral work, or saw their role as clergy. Those who reacted against this may well feel that they wish to avoid doing the same to curates of their own. Unfortunately, this seems to produce a diametrically opposite reaction where no structure or clear expectations of any kind are offered. There is no middle ground, no negotiation. This may be either because negotiation takes time and people feel they are too busy, or because they lack the personal skills to do it; or, as one curate suggested, they fear conflict. This is reinforced by a belief that time spent on organisational matters is time wasted, unnecessary 'admin', not what clergy were ordained for. There is little sense that organisation may be about freeing people to give of their best, find their talents, gain support and confidence, or learn to be self-critical.

CURATES' RELATIONSHIPS WITH INCUMBENTS

The curates were first asked how the relationship with their incumbents developed, and to indicate its good and bad features. To set this in perspective, the twenty interviews indicated that six curates believed their curacies were, or had been, good; four more felt they had been reasonably good, but with significant difficulties or shortcomings; and ten believed their curacies had been essentially unsatisfactory. These are revealing figures, not least because some of the 50 per cent with unsatisfactory curacies had clearly experienced times of great personal unhappiness, or even despair. Since conducting the research I have discussed some of the findings with other clergy; interestingly, a significant number have shown no surprise at these figures, which have often been taken as an opportunity for them to relate similar experiences from their own time as curates. It is comments like these, as much as anything else, which makes me believe that this survey has touched on a very serious and long-standing problem within the Church of England's ordained ministry.

As noted in Chapter 1, a standard response by some senior clergy to complaints of unsatisfactory curacies is to blame the curates for being excessively demanding, hypercritical, or uncharitable towards their colleagues. It is therefore important to record that all the curates I interviewed were at pains to be fair to their incumbents and to seek for mitigating circumstances. There was also a sense that the curates consciously compared their own situations with what fellow curates reported, and often believed themselves to be more fortunate. One commented:

> I know one curate who gets a typed list on Monday mornings from his vicar about what he has to do this week and he has to show that he's done it at the end of the week; and I think, 'I'm glad I haven't got one like that!'

It is also important to acknowledge that several curates felt that their incumbents had been effective in working with them, helping them learn the work of ministry and to be reflective about it. One person described their colleague's approach in some detail. It is worth recording, because it illustrates that good practice can be developed without excessive sophistication or unrealistic amounts of time being given:

> He gave me a discipline . . . and I needed that. . . .
> He had a formula which worked; basically, I wasn't expected to do anything [alone] that I hadn't done before; [so it was] 'You come along and you see it done, then we'd talk about it; then when you and I feel happy you can do either all or part of it with me there, and then we'll talk about it; then when both of us feel happy, you'll do it by yourself and again we'll talk about it.' . . . He did it with absolutely everything; and he was true to his word, so you'd always got the communication, you didn't

feel pushed into doing something, but you also felt
you'd got permission to go to the next thing: but
even then, the communication was still open. . . .
You never felt he wasn't interested. . . . [also] After
I was priested, when it came to celebrating Mass
on Sunday, if one week you did the eight o'clock
and he did the ten, the next week it was the other
way round; if it was Christmas or Easter it made
no difference. There weren't many incumbents, to
listen to my colleagues, who'd give up Midnight
Mass or Easter Sunday.

SOME PATHOLOGIES OF TRAINING

Curates' difficulties with their incumbents fell into certain
distinct categories and it may be helpful to consider them
under the following headings.

1. Lack of preparation before, or feedback after, the task

Some instances of this have been touched upon in Chapter 3
when curates recalled their earliest days in ministry. A significant number concerned funerals, which are both highly
charged pastoral occasions and, for the curate, a very public
arena in which to be operating. Although many curates go
through a 'baptism of fire' by conducting funerals, it has to
be asked whether this is the best way in which to launch
people at the very beginning of their ministries; coping with
bereavement may demand rather more ministerial and pastoral
experience. Moreover, some funerals are more complex than
others:

> It wasn't all that long before he handed me [the
> funeral of] a still-birth; and I said, 'What do I do?
> I've not done one of these before; I've not even got
> a form of service.' But basically he just left me to
> get on with it and I had to find an appropriate

form of service and feel my way round it. There was never any 'How did you get on?'; he didn't ever seem to want to talk through what had gone on afterwards; I didn't actually get any feedback.

Similarly with preaching, as another recalled:

There wasn't much interaction . . . he'd let you preach but there was never any comeback to that, never any response to it, no comment on it; you just did it: which I found very unhelpful. . . . [I mentioned this to him;] his response was, 'We must do something about that', but it never happened. . . . There were always more pressing things [for him] to do.

There was also a more basic aversion to offering comment on how curates were progressing, as another suggested:

I don't get much feedback from him and I *can't* get much feedback from him; if I dig around and ask, 'How am I doing?' – which I asked – 'Oh, fine', but what does that mean? So I don't get a lot of praise and I don't get a lot of criticism; I don't [even] get a lot of bland 'You're doing all right'. On that score, the supervision, training, the guidance with try[ing] it this way, or that way . . . is not there. [He doesn't offer any feedback because] he doesn't like conflict . . . [to offer affirmation] also requires that you say, 'You're not doing very well in that area'; and that runs the risk of [me] saying, 'Rubbish! – back it up.' . . . It's very hard to push for your own supervision . . . you have to know the right questions to ask . . . I almost feel as if I'm expected to know what I don't know in order to ask to know it.

While it is true that offering and receiving critical evaluation can be difficult for both parties, it is also true that processes of conducting supervision have been designed with this in mind and, if used properly, reduce the risk of conflict or of hurting the person so criticised. My own perception is that many clergy have internalised assumptions which seek to avoid conflict at all costs, under the guise of being 'caring', thereby losing any willingness to be truthful. Even so, there is also evidence that clergy can be very negative in criticising their colleagues, as will be seen later.

2. Incumbents' lack of personal organisation and professionalism

A reason frequently cited for lack of helpful preparation and feedback was that the incumbent was too busy. This in turn was often seen as a consequence of an inability to organise their time effectively, though at least one person felt their incumbent was too well organised, but that his organisation excluded the curate. Again, some instances of this have been given in Chapter 3, but the problem is a complex one as these examples illustrate. Incumbents' bad habits could be catching:

> . . . he worked all the time; if he wasn't working he felt guilty. To a considerable extent he transferred that to me; I felt guilty if I wasn't working or if I didn't know what to do next.

Another incumbent was reported to have a more general inability not only to organise himself but to convey a sense of professionalism about his work:

> He's always late for Morning Prayer and I find that very difficult to handle . . . We don't have regular staff meetings at regular times; a professional relationship is lacking . . . we don't work together. . . . It makes it very difficult for me to respect him. I

was here a few weeks when he said one day, 'You put your family first and sod the Church.' I didn't think that was the kind of philosophy which ought to be conveyed [to a newly ordained person] . . . even if there are times one feels that, it can't be a working philosophy. . . . He doesn't give me any time; [because] he's always late there isn't any space. . . . In a staff meeting . . . if someone rings up he won't sit down and [attend to what we are doing].

Another variation on the theme of personal disorganisation was one incumbent's unwillingness to be open about what was expected of the curate:

He often didn't make it clear if he wanted me to be at a particular thing . . . he wouldn't say often until the day whether he expected me to go, or whether he was going, or whether he expected me to go even if he was going. It would come out in questions such as 'What about so-and-so tonight?' or 'Are you able to go?' If two or three days beforehand he'd said, 'There's this coming up; can you manage to go?', you could have made a decision. Sometimes on the day he'd say there was such a thing on in the evening, then just pause; I always knew that what he meant was, 'I want you to go to this', but he never actually said this; non-directive to the nth degree, but actually very manipulative.

Several curates quoted cases of incumbents' failure to communicate information. In most cases this was attributed to forgetfulness, but it was undoubtedly made worse by the frequent lack of proper staff meetings to plan the work of the coming weeks. One curate had clearly become philosophical about this sort of difficulty:

[He's a good incumbent, but] he's not a very good communicator; [even his wife] finds out what's going on by looking in his office. . . . I find out the weddings I'm doing by looking at the list in the choir vestry. . . . I find it frustrating because I'm a person who tries to plan . . . I'm learning now to ask questions . . . to pre-empt him . . . it's my method of coping with it. . . . It's not malicious . . . he's a very busy man. . . . Part of him believes he's told me, but he hasn't . . . [when I tackle him] he's full of apologies. . . . The relationship . . . is not unlike the relationship I had with my boss at work [before ordination]; [I had to] look through papers on his desk or in the diary [to find what was happening]. The training I'm receiving now is not unlike the training I received [then].

Another commented:

[The Vicar] organised a meeting in my front room without telling me . . . I found out when people gave me their apologies that they couldn't come. . . . [His view generally seemed to be] why should I know about things? . . . No communication at all; yet we saw each other twice daily on the whole to say Morning and Evening Prayer.

A further problem was incumbents' inability to manage the boundaries between their work and family life. Several curates commented that incumbents seemed to be more defensive of their own family time than they permitted their colleagues to be; this could become a festering resentment because it could rarely be discussed openly. One instance of family life disrupting work seems particularly bizarre:

He was celebrating Mass and in the middle of the service . . . his bleeper went off – his wife has a bleeper and bleeps him – so he stopped the Mass and went to make a phone call; apparently it wasn't urgent so he came back and carried on. The congregation were livid! . . . when they faced him about it, he said his wife didn't think it was Mass but thought it was Morning Prayer.

Another person believed both that their incumbent's wife made unrealistic demands on him and that he was unable to organise his own priorities:

Maybe [someone] should explain to his partner what having a curate entails; it's not another pair of hands and they won't release [her] husband to do the baby-sitting. . . . He was racked with guilt most of the time that he wasn't doing the job he was supposed to, but his first priority was to his family. It was a destructive situation . . .

There are clearly a number of overlapping issues here, some relating to the ways in which clergy develop bad habits of working in the absence of models of good practice; others arising out of having the family home as the workplace. But what runs through many of these comments on incumbents is a recognition that they seem unable to handle conflicting expectations, from their family, colleagues, work and within themselves. Where such conflicts of expectation arise, it appears that they are usually resolved by ignoring the curate; which in turn undermines the working relationship with them.

3. Unwillingness to share tasks or recognise curates' abilities

One of the ambiguities of curates' ministries is that, although both they and their incumbents are equally authorised by their ordination, the incumbent has both the bishop's authorisation as the principal minister in the parish and generally has more experience than the curate of the work of ministry.

Even so, this is not a static situation, since as curates gain experience they are expected to become, by the end of their curacy, capable of taking sole pastoral charge of a parish for themselves. As noted in Chapter 1, it is also now increasingly common for curates to have skills and experience from employment before ordination – perhaps more, and better authenticated, than the incumbent. This makes counting the curate's years in ordained ministry an unreliable basis for assumptions about their ability. A significant number of interviewees gave instances where they believed incumbents had underestimated their skills, or simply gave them no space in which to learn or exercise their judgement.

> He has a very strong sense that he's here in a leadership role . . . so he has to take things on board for himself . . . [He has to] approve absolutely everything. We started up a music group and tried to sing just one thing a little bit different at the family service; a couple of months ago we did something that wasn't quite in the tradition of the place – now every piece of music has to be approved by [the Musical Director and] him. That gets a little bit frustrating!

Another person, who affirmed their 'admiration and respect' for their incumbent, nonetheless observed:

> The pattern is that [he] has his way and I back down; I've come to realise that he really does believe that, at the end of the day, his ideas are better. . . . He can't take on the role of an assistant with any of his colleagues. . . . I don't think he gets the best out of me. . . . Because he wants to be in control [he believes that] his ideas are the ones which work; sometimes, if I have an exceptional idea, he incorporates my idea into his. . . . He confuses authoritarianism with responsibility.

In recent years there has been much discussion of the ideal of 'collaborative ministry' in the churches, though, as one curate noted, the reality often fell short of the aspiration:

> He tends to use the language of collaboration, but actually keeps things very closely to himself. . . . I don't think he doesn't trust me; he just doesn't share things with me [enough] to get that far.

While it could be argued that these instances were simply a matter of over-cautiousness by incumbents, one curate gave an instance of deliberate plagiarism:

> [There was an adult study group] and he just would not let me lead any of [the sessions]. . . . There was a session when he wanted to do some-thing . . . I said, 'I'd really like to do that; I've done some reading and thinking about that.' He wouldn't let me do it, but I foolishly [lent him an essay I'd done about it at college] . . . He photocopied it and led the session using *my* essay and I wasn't allowed to say anything! [After] things like that I'd just come home *so* angry! . . . I said to him, 'You didn't let me speak', and he said, 'You're not there to talk'.

Once again, there seems to lie behind these instances an unwillingness, or inability, by incumbents to discuss matters of work and responsibility with their colleagues. There appears, too, an over-extensive and rigid assumption about the mean-ing and practice of leadership which may be interpreted as a suspicion that, unless the incumbent is continually defensive of his position, there will be anarchy and chaos. Other curates indicated their incumbents' willingness to allow them space to grow and develop, but these were not as common as instances of restrictiveness and inflexibility. In reality, incumbents probably have little to fear from most curates and laypeople; but the belief that disaster swiftly overtakes those who relax their vigilance, even if only momentarily, dies hard and undermines much of the potential which others seem willing to offer.

4. *Personal remoteness or hostility*

Another paradox of ministry seems to be the inability of many clergy to form even 'workplace' relationships with laypeople or other ministers. This has become more noticeable in recent decades with a renewed emphasis, particularly in the Church of England, on that ill-defined Christian goal of 'fellowship'. Anglican clergy of past ages might often be remote and distant in their dealings with others, while well into the 1960s bishops and archdeacons frequently addressed the 'inferior clergy' by their unadorned surnames. But this is not assumed to be the case today, when many incumbents hope to be known by their Christian names (sometimes to the acute embarrassment of older churchgoers) and even the episcopate have adopted semi-informal titles such as 'Bishop Bill'. A significant number of curates mentioned their lack of personal rapport with their colleagues and this was a source of keen disappointment since those colleagues had often spoken before the curate's ordination of their hopes for close working relationships. One curate admitted:

> On a personal level, I don't know him; all our conversations are around churchy things . . . [the relationship] has not developed as I expected [it would]. I expected it would develop as my relationships with former vicars and clergy had done in the past in parishes I've been in as a layman, where . . . I've got to know them well and they've got to know me well – a depth of trust, even: I don't get to the heart of what he's thinking about some things. . . . I can't imagine going down to the

pub with him, having a pint and talking about all sorts of things. . . . we're not on the same planet.

Another saw a spiritual aspect to this:

> There was no 'hinterland' [to our relationship] I think; and I think that's very important if you're seeing someone every day, if you're praying with someone. I think that's demonstrated in your ministerial experience where being with a congregation for any period of time, you get to know them, particularly any problems, griefs and so on, and this helps you to pray for them and lead worship with them.

It is entirely possible that some of this was due to the incumbents' personalities; surveys of clergy often report a higher than average proportion of introverts and some have claimed that authorised forms of worship and prayer also appeal most to introverted people. What was disturbing was that some of those interviewed believed that their incumbents were unable to handle the consequences of their personalities and projected the problem onto the curate, as here:

> I harbour a suspicion that he has always been frightened of himself and frightened of me. [At first] there was an uneasy peace but this began to break down after a few days; I thought, 'Great, we're making good progress here, he's revealed a bit about himself': but then the next time we'd meet . . . he'd be cold, distant and aloof and I'd think I'd done something wrong. I'd look back and think '. . . what have I done? what's gone wrong here?' and not be able to ask him, '. . . is there something wrong?', because that'd never work. So he just left this awful feeling hanging over you that something had gone wrong, it was your fault, but

it was so bad that you couldn't talk about it. . . . I came to recognise after six months that this was the normal process; he'd revealed more of himself than he was comfortable with and he'd just shut the door on you.

There was also the issue of the curate's popularity:

Initially, I do think he was threatened by having a curate and I was, dare I say it, popular; and curates are, they come and go. . . . He was very poor on praise, very good on criticism.

Despite the comment earlier about many clergy's unwilling-ness to express critical feelings and observations of others, some incumbents could be highly destructive:

When I've felt low it's been because of [his] latest assault; much as you want to laugh it off at the time when someone says all sorts of critical things about you as a person you just wonder, really. . . . If I'd been raising them with somebody, I'd have made a lot of positive comments and then said, 'By the way, do you realise . . .' His approach is to go for the jugular and not give any praise. . . . Recently he more or less told me that he felt the only reason I did anything was just to [annoy him]. . . . We've never had a conversation about the substance of an issue; it's always, '. . . I don't like this, I don't approve of this'.

Even so, there may be affinities between the incumbent unwilling to offer any criticism and the one who attacks others mercilessly; both are ways of keeping people at arm's length and declining to engage constructively with them.

5. *Inappropriate personal attitudes towards the curate*

Possibly the most worrying, and unexpected, area of difficulty reported by curates was their incumbents' capacity to display inappropriate personal attitudes towards them. As the comments below indicate, some of these took the form of treating the curate as though they were their late teenage or early adult children; others had more disturbingly sexual undertones, or were simply intrusive. Although a number of the curates reporting these attitudes were women, men clearly experienced similar difficulties. Clergy are in a sensitive position in their public and professional relationships with others. On one hand there is still a remarkable degree of goodwill and trust shown towards them, even by people who have little to do with the churches. Conversely, this, and the lack of the kinds of professional codes of practice which other occupations would expect, makes them vulnerable both to malicious accusations, and also to the risk of their own self-control and integrity failing them. It must be said that some clergy place themselves at risk by unprofessional behaviour and others may simply be inept at handling their personal relationships. These problems are clearly experienced by curates, as one commented:

> I don't find it an easy relationship . . . I dislike talking to him on a very personal level because he does have this knack of probing further than I want to go. . . . I made him aware of that; I told him . . . it was getting a bit too much and he did accept that. . . . [For example] he always asked me how I spent my day off; [I told him,] 'I don't want you to ask me this, it's my day off; it's actually none of your business what I do.' . . . It may just have been a general concern [for me] . . . but it didn't *feel* like that; it felt intrusive.

Two women reported being treated as though they were

their incumbents' children:

> There were times – and I used to tell him as well . . .
> when I used to think, 'You're my parish priest, I'm
> working with you, we're colleagues, but somehow
> it's like you're my father and I don't want that' . . .
> [I felt pushed into that;] it was [a relationship] he
> could handle; he had a teenage daughter he got on
> with well, he could cope with that.

Another recalled that the problem seemed to include the
incumbent's wife:

> [Before I got engaged] he said to me several times,
> 'You can come and spend Saturday evenings with
> us, you're just a couple of years older than my son';
> there was [the implication that] it was all going to be
> lovely, we'll look after her, she'll be like another
> daughter. When they realised I wasn't a daughter-
> type person, I was a sexual human being, they
> changed dramatically, particularly his wife . . . [to
> begin with] it may just have been generous talk, but
> it never quite *felt* like that. . . . I never went: I was
> never invited again when - - - appeared on the scene.

Men were also subject to this process:

> [He] has a perception that . . . one day I'll grow out
> of [my ideas] he thinks I'm inconsistent . . . like a
> wayward son. . . . [Someone commented] that they
> felt that he thought when I first came here that I'd
> be putty in his hands . . . when it became obvious
> that I wouldn't be like that [the other person]
> thought he changed his attitude toward me.

Another used the parent/child relationship in a more
metaphorical sense:

> On the professional level I was still trying to be the
> good child, not creating divisions and loyalty being
> paramount . . . but trying to tread on eggshells
> everywhere I went and not upsetting the apple-cart,
> gradually getting more and more worn down.

All the above might be thought to be misdirected attempts either at showing personal concern for a junior colleague, or else a tendency to adopt a father-like role in dealing with problems. Such an understanding might see any fault on the incumbents' part as simply a matter of being overly paternalistic, or patronising. More difficult is the following:

> He came out with an awful statement about 'I'm a
> man, you're a woman; I've talked to my wife about
> this' – I knew what he was trying to say – 'If I say
> it, perhaps that'll mean it won't happen; but there
> is the possibility of us jumping into bed with each
> other.' I thought, 'Give me some credit!' I just
> couldn't believe it.

The kindest judgement on such a statement is that it was a serious gaffe; but it might equally be interpreted as an oblique sexual proposal, or even sexual harassment which is actionable. One wonders whether similar 'warnings' were made to women church members, or women with whom the incumbent had pastoral relationships. Nor is it unique; when another woman's incumbent asked her whether she was a lesbian, she sensibly told him it was none of his business.

What this may reveal is another aspect of the problems clergy have in maintaining appropriate personal boundaries in their work; just as time management may be undermined by allowing family concerns to intrude into work, so attempts are made to co-opt colleagues into the family. Unfortunately, the nature of ordained ministry makes this more possible than might be the case elsewhere; but it certainly is of concern to curates.

ARE INCUMBENTS ALL BAD?

In view of the comments above, it would be tempting to think the answer was 'yes'. In reality, most curates, including those who had experienced serious difficulties, were often happy to acknowledge their colleagues' strengths and abilities. A significant number of people confirmed that they felt they had enjoyed working with incumbents on occasions, or that there had been times when they felt they were getting on well, even if this did not last very long. Some genuinely liked, or even admired, their incumbents. Several said they got on well enough with them, even if they were difficult to work with, often through being disorganised or over-busy. Several of those who were interviewed after they had left their curacies told how they still kept in touch with their former incumbents and enjoyed their occasional meetings with them at clergy gatherings.

What was equally clear was that far too many incumbents had little idea of how to form good and beneficial working relationships with their curates and that, despite good intentions and high expectations, this all too often failed to happen. In most cases curates found that once they had been assumed to have mastered the rudiments of preaching, conducting public worship and rites of passage, plus a limited pastoral repertoire of sick and bereavement visiting, incumbents effectively abandoned them to do whatever they gave them, or to find projects of their own. ('Assumed' is an important word here; for example, several people said their incumbents had never seen them conduct a funeral on their own.) There was little or no sense of working together, no mutual interest in their work, no sense of their efforts being 'owned' by the church or their colleagues. Some people managed to cope, or even thrive, on this and several people related how they found they had particular interests or aptitudes for work they took up, to the point of wanting to concentrate on this in future appointments. But there was little or no sense that they were being trained for present or future ministry and often a feeling that their expectations at the start of their ministries had been badly disappointed.

OTHER CLERGY

Interviewees were also asked how they got on with other clergy, including those who worked with them and their incumbents. On the whole people were positive about these rather more distant colleagues and several indicated that they felt they had been able to discuss relations with their incumbents with other people who offered sympathy, comfort and advice. The knowledge that, as one person put it, 'they know what the boss is like', was important in allowing them to retain a sense of proportion about problems. Significantly, two of those who were badly dissatisfied with their curacies reported that there were neither other clergy working in the parish nor was there much contact with clergy beyond the parish, in one case because they lived a long way from the cathedral city and therefore found diocesan gatherings difficult to attend.

The benefits of relating to other clergy were not directly related to the times when the curates had contact with them. Even occasional meetings could help diffuse feelings of frustration or disappointment, and older clergy might be helpful sources of wisdom and advice. One person told how, when they first arrived in the parish, their incumbent tried to enlist them on his side in a dispute with another minister; the curate refused and came to find the third person a source of help and encouragement, even though they had little in common. It was clear that some people also found other clergy easier to work with than their incumbent, including the man who observed:

> The three who work best together are [two women] and myself. . . . I don't feel in competition with my female colleagues . . . [but] I feel there is competitiveness and rivalry amongst [men] and that does

91

affect how much one allows others to encroach and support. [With women] there's something about vulnerability and using the strength of others for the good of all.

Competitiveness was a factor mentioned by a number of curates, who experienced it not only in relations with other clergy, but sometimes with lay readers in the parish. It is possible that some of the difficulties with incumbents discussed above were motivated by similar attitudes. While competitiveness is to be found in many other work situations, it may be more difficult to work with in a church context because there is an expectation that there everyone is united in a common cause.

Anglican parishes are grouped geographically into deaneries, the clergy of which gather for periodic 'chapter' meetings, presided over by the rural dean, the bishop's appointee, who is also an incumbent in the deanery. (In urban locations, the term 'area dean' is sometimes used.) Chapters are intended to be business meetings for the clergy, but may also be places for some education, discussion and mutual support. Some curates found chapter meetings, and the individuals they encountered there, to be helpful and encouraging and a few reported that the rural dean had taken a supportive interest in them. Others found that chapters contained too many people who either took no interest in them, or were perceived to be 'on another wavelength'. One woman reported:

> The other clergy in the deanery were all deeply patronising; 'Oh, you're - - -'s curate aren't you? We've all heard about you and your short skirts': 'I'd quite fancy a curate, especially one that runs round like a whippet!' . . . It was very difficult to know how to respond to that, apart from telling them where to go!

Once again this interviewee's comments indicate an understandable range of reactions to other clergy. One or two commented that they found ecumenical clergy gatherings more helpful than Anglican events, at least one directly attributing this to the sense that there was less competitiveness than in the deanery.

Some curates clearly found kindred spirits with whom to talk, sometimes a welcome contrast to their incumbent. Others failed to do so and this occasionally contributed to a greater sense of isolation and abandonment. Much of this is a reflection of the intermittent success with which attempts to get clergy to work and talk together are rewarded and the curates' experience is not particularly different from the reactions of other clergy throughout the Church of England; which itself confirms that they may be a fairly representative sample of ministers.

POST-ORDINATION TRAINING

The recognition that curates may need particular kinds of support, as well as in-service training, is the rationale behind post-ordination training (POT). In the Church of England this is provided by all dioceses and is compulsory for all those in the first three years of ordained ministry, though exactly what is provided, and how it is structured and serviced, varies considerably between dioceses. Essentially POT is intended to provide a structure for training in the early years in which the focus moves between learning 'on the job' in the parish and diocesan-organised events which bring curates together, either into local groups or for diocesan-wide occasions. There is also generally a personal support structure which may involve peer support (e.g. in 'cell groups'); or more managerial or pastoral involvements with a 'tutor' or 'mentor', a 'senior friend' or a spiritual director approved, if not appointed, by the diocese; or a combination of these. Most people were positive about at least some aspects of POT:

> I've found it a great support and source of release.
> . . . It's an opportunity to get together and let off
> steam about the latest problem with the incumbent;
> and being with people who are at the same stage of
> ministry.

Again:

> . . . the group we've had has gelled very, very, well;
> it's got a fairly wide experience of churchmanship
> and background . . . the group has worked phenom-
> enally well together. . . . [Meeting together] has
> been its greatest benefit and it has been designed
> so as to allow ample time for that.

Further questions revealed that most people saw the main
usefulness of POT as being a peer-support structure where
they could meet up with other curates away from their incumbents and have space to discuss and compare experiences.
Conversely there was much less enthusiasm for POT as an
educational process:

> . . . the only use [of POT] was that we got together
> at the beginning as a group and talked about our
> experiences . . . and one or two friendships devel-
> oped out of that, which was helpful for support; . . .
> [I] could meet up with friends, but I could have
> done that in the pub.

The main criticisms of POT as a learning process were (a)
that it often duplicated work done in training before ordination; (b) that learning events were often poorly presented, or
inadequately prepared; (c) that there was little flexibility in
what people did in POT and a failure to recognise experience and skills gained prior to ordination; and (d) that the
subjects covered often reflected more the presuppositions

and hobby-horses of the organisers (including, sometimes, other curates) than the realities of the ministries in which people were engaged. Several people who expressed such criticisms also indicated a certain sympathy with those responsible for overseeing the POT process in the diocese, some of whom did so on a part-time basis only or as a small part of a diverse portfolio of responsibilities. One person recalled asking the director of POT what were the aims of the process, to be given the embarrassed reply that there were none. There were also mixed feelings about the value of giving people tutors or mentors with whom to work; though some people commented very positively on the enthusiasm and commitment of year or group tutors.

Criticisms of POT reflect the more general difficulties of providing in-service training in an organisation without the operational objectives which define in-service training goals in other occupations. This in turn reflects the often ill-defined expectations about the purpose of ministry in the churches, beyond coping with day-to-day tasks and keeping the wheels turning. It may also reflect an excessively inward-looking and personalised concept of what being a Christian minister involves, which makes outwardly identifiable objectives and skills hard to address. But the specific problems of POT may also be bound up with the failures of so many incumbent/curate relationships at even the most basic functional level. People feeling disappointed by their lack of an elementary working partnership may need help and support from others before they can engage with learning or critical reflection on their work. From personal experience I can confirm that POT as a learning process is often undermined by the need to cope with curates' anxieties, disappointments and anger at the ways they have been treated, while centrally organised training cannot rely upon more basic training being offered in the parish. Poor practice by training incumbents effectively sabotages a whole range of training for curates, as well as harming them personally.

BISHOPS AND SENIOR CLERGY

Bishops are more aware now than in the past of the difficulties faced by curates and it is encouraging to see that they often make special efforts to offer support and help to them. Bishops are in any event expected to be 'pastors to the pastors', though this must be set alongside other more managerial and judicial functions which may lead to role confusions unless handled carefully. The interviewees were asked about their attitudes towards bishops, archdeacons and other senior diocesan staff, and, bearing in mind their difficulties with incumbents, whether they would feel they could approach them to talk over any problems they had.

The curates varied in their responses. Most felt that they could talk with at least one member of the diocese's senior staff about certain kinds of difficulties, though most realised that there were areas of concern which it would be imprudent to raise. Their perceptions of bishops were mixed, though interestingly a number of people thought their diocesan bishops might be more approachable than suffragans. These variations were partly a product of the contact curates had with bishops; several women felt that they were better known to bishops than their male colleagues, if only because there were less women in the diocese. Some also felt that their bishop had been supportive of women in ministry in the wake of the 1992 General Synod vote to ordain them as priests. On the other hand, several curates expressed the sense that they neither knew their bishop, nor were known by them, sufficiently to talk about anything at a deep level. A few commented that they had been wary of approaching the bishop with a problem, but that when they did so he had been very understanding and supportive. One person was very positive about efforts made on their behalf by the senior staff:

> Pastorally, if there's a problem [they] are there, all guns blazing, doing their utmost . . . Their job . . .

> was to help me get back together again and get on
> with the vocation I felt I had. . . . The diocesan
> bishop and his team are very good in that situation.
> . . . I felt secure [because] the bishop meant business
> and that it was all OK.

In some dioceses one of the bishops has a particular responsibility for curates, which could be beneficial in unexpected ways:

> When we were on retreat [fellow curates and I]
> were putting our heads together and finding out . . .
> that [at a certain time] we'd all been taken for a
> supervision session by our training vicars, which
> we thought was quite a remarkable coincidence.
> Then we found out that the bishop had sent round
> a right snorter of a letter . . . we think he'd twigged
> that [supervision] didn't quite happen so [the
> incumbents] were told to get on with it. [When I
> met the bishop] he said, 'You're not there as another
> pair of hands; you're there to be trained.'

Conversely, a number of people were wary of encounters with
bishops and archdeacons:

> I don't trust most of them – really: I don't know
> where they're coming from. I feel very much that
> curates seem to get treated almost as nobodies in
> practical terms, they're not people you should con-
> sult . . . and I play my cards very close to my chest
> when I'm talking to those sorts of people. . . . Having
> said that . . . I do quite like the [diocesan] bishop
> . . . there's no pomposity [about him] and you don't
> feel uncomfortable . . . but there are lots of things I
> wouldn't get into talking to him about.

Again:

Oh, no . . . I don't think I really could talk with my
local archdeacon or my local bishop; I think the
archdeacon was appointed . . . because he was very
good at chairing committees [and] it's very clear
that that's his element. I don't really feel I could
have sufficient confidence in my local bishop to feel
free to talk with him . . . Amongst my colleagues,
some like the bishop more than I do, but I don't
think that gets translated into . . . going and having
a deep and meaningful conversation with him.

One woman recalled:

The few times I met [the Archdeacon] at particular
'do's' he could be rude . . . he always focused on
what I wore, or my earrings – dire! The only time I
had to go and see him, he had to sign my car loan
[application]; he wasn't at all helpful. He [inferred]
it could be a problem – nonsense! you can get a
car loan easily from the Church Commissioners; I
know that now, but I didn't then; he made me suffer
a bit before he was willing to sign it. I think he did
this to other people; to other women, I'm sure.

Several people commented that they had talked with senior
staff who had been willing to listen, but, beyond expressing
sympathy, were clearly unwilling to do anything. Some people
thought this was because, as one put it, 'They don't like hassle';
others that the bishops felt that 'getting things off your chest'
was sufficient. Several interviewees believed that this belied
a lack of proper structures for dealing with problems and
grievances:

There was no clear mechanism of anyone to talk to
[about problems]; there was an assumption that it
would never really happen . . . the system didn't

> seem to work . . . if it got that bad then you had to go and talk to [diocesan staff] and the curate would lose out if it came to a conflict – like a car and a hedgehog – there was no way the curate was going to win; the curate would be got rid of as a problem. *[A view apparently supported by evidence from within the diocese]*

Or as another person put it:

> You have to go and look for [help] . . . as long as you appear to be coping, no one ever looks to see whether you are; as long as you give the appearance [of coping] that's fine . . . [unless you have the confidence to ask] you could sink without trace – well . . . they'd probably notice the bubbles!

It is too early to draw any overall conclusions about the material in this chapter; this will come in Chapter 6. It is important to note at this point the considerable breadth, as well as depth, of the problems reported by the interviewees and the often worrying sense of frustration, anger and despair which lay behind what they mentioned. Perhaps the most telling comment on their training as curates was the frequency with which they told me, 'This is the first time anyone has talked to me about this' – despite some having been ordained for four or five years. Even the most elementary supervision would have made this impossible.

CHAPTER 5

Families, friends, finance
and the future

It was only after coming [to my first incumbency]
that I began to think, 'Yes, full-time ministry *is* for
me', because [I had] serious doubts as a curate –
which I hadn't really had before. It just seemed so
limited and I thought, 'Can I spend the next thirty-
five years doing this?'

Whereas the preceding chapters have concentrated on the
curates themselves and their professional activities, here the
discussion encompasses their domestic and social lives, and
also considers their expectations for the future. In Chapter 2
mention was made of the considerable influences which
ordinands' families' interests have on their choice of job, but
the nature of ordained ministry means that families have a
continuing involvement in the clergy's work in ways that
might not be the case with other professionals. This might
broadly be due to three main factors which will be considered
in detail below. First, that the nature of the church is such as
to involve families in its life in a way that would not be the
case of a lawyer or a surgeon, for example. Not only can families
go to church, but there is a powerful expectation that they will
do so, often reinforced by the common emphasis on family
life, as reflected in worship entitled 'family communion', 'family
service', or the ideal of the church as a family. The second
factor is that stipendiary parish clergy live in tied housing,
the occupancy of which is a mandatory part of their conditions
of service, and this housing provides not only accommodation
but also work space, the demands of which can, and do,

impinge upon everyone living there. The third factor is money, or often the lack of it. At the time these interviews were conducted most curates received an annual stipend of around £13,000, varying slightly between dioceses, which might rise to around £14,000 for incumbents. Unlike other occupations, once clergy become incumbents there are virtually no incremental payments reflecting additional responsibilities or years of service: cathedral staff, archdeacons and bishops do receive higher salaries, but there are relatively few such posts.[1] Although a house is provided for the time a minister is in paid ministry, there is not the opportunity to buy a house to which they can retire unless they are willing to have a 'second home' which they do not occupy full time. Clergy stipends have improved over the years since the time in the 1960s when some curates were reported to be living below supplementary benefit level, but, as will be seen, the material reward for the job, even taking the house into account, may be much less than in other occupations.

The position of clergy families has changed over the years. As noted in Chapter 1, a major difference from thirty years ago is that very many ordinands are married and have children before they begin training. Selection, training and ordination can have a powerfully disruptive effect on families, and the minister's public role after ordination can fundamentally impinge on marital partners and children. Clergy wives, like married women generally, have gained a degree of emancipation to the point where they often go out to work and are no longer expected to stay at home to be an 'unpaid curate'. But if the oppressive drudgery depicted in George Orwell's *A Clergyman's Daughter*[2] is a thing of the past, clergy wives may still feel adversely defined by their husbands' work and parishioners' expectations, a theme explored in at least two recent televised productions, Alan Bennett's *Bed Among the Lentils* and Joanna Trollope's *The Rector's Wife*.[3] They may also feel encouraged by others to play an active part in the congregations where their husbands work; or may wish to do so. Interestingly, clergy husbands seem to have few such expectations placed upon them.

FAMILY AND FRIENDS

To discover something of the ways in which ordained ministry impinged upon curates' families, the interviewees were asked whether their close relatives' and friends' attitudes towards them had been changed by ordination; and whether this was also the case with more distant relatives and friends. They were also asked whether they felt that their ability to form new friendships had been affected since ordination, reflecting a concern that clergy may feel personally isolated by their role.

Most interviewees reported little change in relationships with close family and friends. This was often explained in terms of the length of time over which they had been actively considering ordained ministry, or had been in training – a period of up to eight or ten years in some cases. However, two people reported difficulties of perception by their close relatives:

> [Family and friends] simply do not, even to this day, fully appreciate the nature of my work. Even Christian family members and friends who go to church don't really know what I'm about. . . . They're still stuck in the, 'only works one hour a week' syndrome . . . [I can feel] marginalised within a marginalised sect; it's as if I've been transformed into something people simply can't grasp hold of.

Another said of their parents:

> They didn't really understand why I wished to be ordained . . . there had been distinct hostility. . . . My saving grace was that I [was] one of the first women and [this] made it kosher . . . they told all their friends, not that I was being priested, but

that I was one of the first women . . . as long as I
was doing something for the first time as a woman
and against the establishment, that was wonderful!

A further aspect, commented upon by several people who had
been members of Free Churches before becoming Anglicans,
was that their families sometimes had difficulty in coming to
terms with the particular ethos of Anglican ministry. Even
so, there was often a sense of pride in what the curates had
achieved and the feeling of admiration for a life dedicated to
Christian service.

Curates' children, particularly teenagers, could view their
fathers' new career with misgivings, if not embarrassment, as
one person observed:

It doesn't give you a lot of street cred round here
to have a dad who's a vicar; when our boys first
went to their secondary school people asked them,
'What does your dad do?' and they were going
round telling everybody I was a bus driver.

There was also the matter of clerical dress . . .

Initially the closest family found it difficult when I
started wearing the gear; there was a degree of perception change, in spite of all the preparation . . .
[my daughter] saw my dog-collar at my ordination
and said, 'Does that thing come off?'

. . . though there could be unexpected reactions:

One thing that helped [me] a lot was my eldest
daughter; [before ordination] she had said, 'If you
think I'm going to walk down the street with you
wearing [your collar] you can think again.' . . . On
the day of my ordination it all got a bit claustro-
phobic and I said I was going out for a walk; my

elder daughter said, 'Can I come out with you?' and walked down the street with me. . . . That still sticks . . . the lack of embarrassment and the acceptance I felt . . . was a really big thing.

Several people commented on ways in which their families' privacy was sometimes intruded upon:

I'm a lot more public property and people feel they can make observations to [my wife] about me and about her that they wouldn't to ordinary people . . . if comments like that were made about people who don't go to church they might punch them on the nose! . . . [for example] there's interest in your sex life – it's never actually put in those terms – 'When are you having children?' [or] 'Well, ministers always have a lot of children, don't they?' and you think . . . 'I've never invited you to comment on things like this.'

Curates' wider family and more distant friends were the most likely to change their attitudes, or at least be uncertain how to relate to them after ordination. Only one person reported that a friendship had foundered as a result of ordination, but others indicated that their church membership, often over a long period, had marked them out in some way amongst friends who showed no great surprise to hear that they had been ordained. A number of curates also found themselves in demand to officiate at family rites of passage, which might unexpectedly enhance their standing among relatives:

Shortly after I was ordained deacon my nephew died at the age of twenty . . . and they wanted me to play some part in the service. I'd done one funeral and I was extremely reluctant to do this, particularly as it was up in - - -. . . . I was prevailed upon and in

the end I agreed to do it. It was a great relief to the
family. . . . I found it very difficult; there were 200-
300 people there . . . I think that made me realise
they saw me differently . . . I was somebody who
belonged to the family, who needed to do this for the
family. I was glad I did it and I got a lot of support
from all sorts of people in doing it.

Having a minister in the family or circle of friends might also
have a certain novelty value, which some people found more
difficult to handle, suspecting sometimes that it could be a
form of stereotyping in parallel to the attitudes of the public
towards clergy. One commented:

Being a woman there is a sort of strippogram aspect
to it – I have been asked if I was a strippogram
[while I was waiting] at the station; I said, 'That's
my church over there' – I never saw them again!

Another factor in family life was the possibility of taking time
off from work when there is no workplace to leave behind at
the end of the day. Curates are supposed to have a full day
off each week and six weeks' annual holiday, including five
Sundays, though several commented on the problem of taking
time off at home:

We've found that we can't really holiday by staying
in the house; there are continuous interruptions so
we've tended to draw on our savings [in order to be
able to go away].

There were also difficulties about what to do with leisure time
during the week, as a woman observed:

Most of the other single ministers of my acquaintance are young men for whom an evening off might
involve going down to the pub and meeting friends

there; that's not easily an option for a single woman, especially not here.

It may be that there are particular aspects to leisure for clergy, which might be shared with those whose work involves a good deal of contact with people. The time use survey revealed that most curates' leisure did not involve them in membership of organisations, or in some kind of organised activity. This may be because clergy simply are not 'joiners'; but it may also be because group leisure pursuits are rather too much like work to offer much relaxation. There may be a personality element in this too, though more often it would appear to be explained by curates' need to work at evenings and weekends when others are at leisure. Given the often considerable part the church had played in curates' lives before ordination there might also be a sense that they had lost an important leisure activity by opting to work for it and this did not seem to have been replaced by anything else. The need to work in others' leisure time also made it difficult to maintain existing friendships; one person commented that they lived in the same street as a friend for twelve months without being able to find time to meet socially. Although no one complained of isolation or loneliness, it is easy to see how this can happen to some clergy.

The most obvious group to whom clergy might relate socially is the church membership. In the past there has been a culture which discouraged making friends with people living in the parish, whether churchgoers or not, partly on the grounds that such relationships might compromise ministers' authority over others; or might indicate favouritism; or that for those thus 'set apart' certain recreations might be undesirable, even though they were acceptable enough for lay people. There is an undeclared assumption that clergy, like other middle-class professionals, will have their own circle of friends and acquaintances drawn from university, or family, or professional contacts. These relationships would be conducted over a wider geographical area than the parish and, since those involved would be the clergy's social equals, would make relationships with parishioners, who might be social inferiors, unnecessary. It must be said that, as in much of English life, class considerations are significant here; the idea that one ought not to have friendships in the parish has to this day not inhibited clergy from joining Rotary Clubs, Masonic Lodges or being chaplains to the local Conservative Association.

Few of the interviewees seemed to espouse the view that they ought not to have friends among the church membership, though one person commented:

> I don't have friends in the parish; I made that a conscious decision when I started. There are people I'd like to continue to see after [leaving] but probably won't [because] I doubt if they or I could get out of . . . me being a minister. . . . I think there is a necessary distance required in the role which cannot be broached and, whatever they say, [people] want that distance because they can demand things, rightly and properly . . . which would be outrageous from a friend.

Another was conscious of possible favouritism:

> I think it's to do with boundaries. The boundaries which exist between friends are different from the boundaries which exist when you're standing in a pastoral relationship with somebody; people who you're not friendly with see you with other members of the congregation and they can easily see that the boundaries are different and it's there that tension arises. . . . I suppose they would characterise it [as favouritism].

Some people reported having been wary of making friends of parishioners initially, though they later changed their minds:

> I have some friends in the parish; I came as their
> curate but now that's a minor part of the friendship.
> . . . [I'm not bothered by making friends in the
> parish] any more [because of] going through my
> first year with very few friends and really getting
> quite low; I thought, 'This is crazy', so then I opened
> up a bit more.

In general curates recognised that their friendships with
parishioners were similar to other friendships made in the
workplace before ordination. They were focused in the work
context and, while important, were often thought unlikely to
survive the curate's move to another job. There were, they
recognised, degrees of intensity in friendship:

> I've made one or two good friendships with people
> since coming to the parish; they're parishioners,
> they're in the congregation . . . I may be wary what
> I say to them, but I'm wary what I say to all my
> friends; as I'm not one to disclose everything to
> them, it's been no hardship. . . . Part of me wonders
> whether I should or not, but they're good friend-
> ships . . . not a bar or hindrance to my ministry. . . .
> I suppose they are very much a friendship in what
> I'm doing . . . often it's on a church footing that I
> see them anyway.

Some people saw friendship as a *motif* in ministry:

> To be open to people as a clergyperson may be a
> sacrifice and they see that and value it; because of
> that willingness to be friendly or open they too
> respond and friendship can develop with a person
> at a level that I've found to be an extraordinary
> privilege. Because of that, I don't see parishioners
> as clients or customers, but as people who befriend

. . . befriending is always a two-way process; it's always been my experience that whatever I've given to people they've more than returned.

A consequence of curates' family life was that children often brought parents into contact with other parents. Several people spoke appreciatively of acquaintances and friendships struck around the school gate, or at playgroups or other children's activities. Similarly with childminding arrangements, though these might cause complications:

A woman in the congregation came to look after [our child], which created problems for [her] among her peers; she gets snide comments about being my favourite – I must say she plays up to it slightly – I don't think she's miserable about it, but I do see it as a problem for me . . . I wouldn't want [other people] to think I related in a special way to [her] which excluded them.

As noted in Chapter 2, some curates had opted to work in areas of deprivation and here questions of class and social expectations clearly played a significant part in forming even working relationships:

There are several things involved. Firstly, people are nervous about inviting 'The Minister' because their home might not be good enough; I might expect something special of them which they couldn't put on – which hadn't crossed my mind when I first came here! Secondly, people don't invite [others] to meals . . . everybody with whom I've had a meal . . . when I've gone it's been a special occasion, pulling out all the stops, not just cheese on toast. . . . It was made clear by one or two people that [being invited to my home] wasn't expected . . .

partly because when I came I felt there was a certain amount of feeling that some people had been invited to the vicarage and other people hadn't, if I . . . invited people . . . others would say, 'I haven't been invited, what's wrong with me?'

The interviewees were also asked whether they felt that ordination had affected their ability to make new friendships. A number commented that attempts to do so had to overcome assumptions and stereotypes which people often had of clergy. One woman observed:

I don't think it's a great turn-on if you go out to a night club and you meet a bloke who asks, 'What do you do for a living?' and you say, 'I'm a priest [or deacon] in the Church of England'!

Others had adopted subterfuges . . .

I have had to spend quite careful time helping people to get over the slight embarrassment of the fact that I'm a priest. I [recently] joined a choir; I was a member for about three months before I let on, because I wanted people to know me as *me* . . . because people have preconceptions.

. . . while another was more pessimistic:

You have to live a lie and not tell anyone what you do; or spend several hours telling people what you do and all about it, which I think probably I can't be bothered to do.

It was also clear that the period of time for which curates expected to be working in a place affected their calculations:

I suppose at the back of my mind I'm thinking, 'Well, we'll not be here that long', and because we're near to where we used to live we're not short of friends; in fact it's the other way round.

The counsel that clergy ought not to befriend parishioners is often based on the possibility of compromising their ministerial authority in relation to others. It is significant that several people noted the converse in relations with other people, who seemed unwilling to allow them to drop the clerical role. One person was philosophical:

It's a bit like if you're a doctor, people have to tell you what their [medical] conditions are . . . people say, 'Oh, I haven't been to church since Adam was a boy', or, 'I went to a baptism last week'. . . . They're nervous and have to show that they know something about who you are and what you do.

Another woman was less so:

I went and had a massage; they knew when I arrived that I was a priest, so the woman who gave me the massage – which I had to pay for – spent the entire forty minutes telling me about her disabled son and her relationship with the Seventh Day Adventists; so I felt physically renewed but spiritually and mentally exhausted by the time I got out! I can't say, 'I don't want to talk about this' – or perhaps I should? – but you have to absorb all this which they want you to absorb. To become friends with someone you have to get through all that, which is very difficult. . . . I am a priest, I don't want to take that off, but I want to be a human being as well.

As the interviews progressed it became clear that the matter of friendships was, unsurprisingly, a complex one. Much depended on people's personalities, the ways in which their families functioned – some were more self-contained than others – the nature of the social context in which people worked, which offered certain dominant patterns of socialisation, and simple opportunity. One person indicated that making new friends had been possible and productive:

> I've [made] a lot of friends within the - - - movement . . . wonderful people who've got nothing to do with religion at all! . . . I would hope that in the next post I will be able to get out far more and have much more of a social life. . . . So much of my energy was taken up with just existing [here] for the first two years that there wasn't space for that.

This observation points to another factor; friendships old and new take time to cultivate and maintain and this may be in short supply as people embark on a new career. Even if work patterns permit, unless they are particularly motivated, curates may feel too tired at the end of a day's work to go out and meet people or join groups. This is no doubt common to other people; except that they may use weekends for socialising. Other occupational groups may have to contend with public stereotypes of their work, or the tendency of those they meet to engage them in 'professional' conversations; this may be why teachers or doctors or undertakers might be more likely to socialise with others in the same occupation. For clergy, the increasing emphasis on friendship within churches, noted in Chapter 4, may incline people to see no harm in befriending the minister; indeed the idea that they are 'human, just like us' and not distant or aloof may be a powerful attraction. Considering their disappointments and problems with training incumbents, none of the interviewees seemed to be desperate to befriend others at all costs. But the quality of supportive friendships with people within and beyond the congregation may throw curates' difficulties with incumbents into sharper relief: why is it so difficult to get on with the vicar when people who never go to church are so friendly? One person expressed the feelings of many interviewees:

> [The effect of ordination] has been more positive than negative; it's enabled me to have some relationships that I wouldn't have been able to have otherwise, perhaps. My personality compensates for the fact that I'm ordained in some respects . . . people seem to feel that I'm an OK person to talk to . . . people have invited me to be involved in some things which I wouldn't have been invited to be if I'd not been ordained.

FINANCE

Attention has already been drawn to the generally modest levels of payment for clergy, even allowing that they are housed free of rent or Council Tax charges. But discussions of clergy remuneration involve more than payments in cash or kind. During the early 1990s the Church Commissioners, the central body responsible for paying clergy in the Church of England, admitted that around £800 million had been lost from the value of its property portfolio. This in turn accelerated the trend towards an increasing proportion of clergy stipends being funded by the dioceses, which are in turn funded by individual parishes. There was much talk at the time of the possibility of some clergy being unable to find jobs, despite total numbers of clergy falling throughout the period. Although this situation appears to have stabilised recently – though it is notoriously difficult to obtain very clear information on this point – clergy are beginning to recognise that the uncertainties of employment suffered by many other people in the last two decades may not have passed them by.

In view of these trends, interviewees were asked what material difference they felt ordination had made to them; and also how they now viewed their future material security. A major factor affecting responses to the first question was whether the curate had become established in an occupation before commencing training for ordination. Those who had been students, or had just started in some other line of work were most positive, as one person observed:

> Overnight I became wealthy in a way I had never been before: to have £800 a month to spend entirely on myself I had never had before; it is a large sum of money . . . it's wonderful; I have a superb house and lots of things are taken care of . . . [but] I'd never had a salary of eleven or twelve thousand pounds: though my friends have salaries three times that!

The latter point about comparisons with friends and contemporaries was echoed by a number of curates:

> There's the age-old problem with clergy; you have the social status and the professional status, which is higher than your material income. My friends who are solicitors and accountants, with the same degree as me, are all on £30,000 or more each, and there's two of them!

For those longer-established in another job before ordination there were obvious comparisons between earnings then and now; but also expectations of future salary levels now needed revision:

> One thing that does make a difference is knowing that between now and retirement my standard of living won't improve at all; that's unusual for so-called professional people. . . . In the job I was in

before there was an expectation of promotion and increments . . . [and] that does influence decisions about longer-term expenditure.

Reimbursement of working expenses is a further area of financial concern for clergy. The Church's assumption is that costs incurred in the exercise of their ministries should be reimbursed to clergy by the parishes where they work. Because such a situation places clergy in direct negotiation with church councils there can be all sorts of complications. Some clergy find it difficult to get parishes to see expenses as a legitimate charge; others discover that poorer parishes may find these difficult or impossible to pay, even if they want to. On the other hand there is a long-standing tradition that clergy will be dispensers of money to those in need, or to the church for its own purposes. Once again, social class has moulded many expectations in both these areas. The affluent middle-class professional clergyman might hitherto have been expected to have inherited wealth or unearned income which would make expenses of office superfluous and allow him to give to the needy and make substantial contributions to parish expenditure. Although there have long been many poorly paid clergy, particularly curates, these old expectations can still bear heavily on the present, as one person in an inner-city parish observed:

It's quite a poor parish . . . [there was] quite a lot of questioning about expenses, and why should the curate be able to charge going to church to the parish when the congregation can't. There was a sense of guilt put upon you that you were a charge on the parish. . . . I [also] feel pressure upon me to take a lead in giving to the church, so while I've been here most of my giving has actually gone to the church whereas before it was shared out among other agencies.

Much more affluent parishes might also be a problem, however:

> [I divide my giving among the churches] and even in one of the wealthiest parishes . . . my contribution is higher than the highest giving; this causes some friction in the household because it means we don't have a holiday, basically! . . . One of the parishes is extremely wealthy; we did have two cars, [one] a rusty old heap which I used to pool around in, which finally died and which we can't replace [because] we'd used the last of our savings to get it. . . . I happened to mention this and the person said, 'Oh, you'll be able to get another one, won't you?' – but what with? . . . They don't perceive how difficult it is.

Living in a tied house could be a mixed blessing. Several people commented that they appreciated their house, but felt concerned that it wasn't theirs and that the security for the future represented by owning a house of their own was absent just as jobs began to look less secure. Several people commented adversely on the standards to which the houses they occupied were maintained . . .

> We don't have any say where we live and there are things which need doing in this house and we can't afford to do them; the carpets are awful and the windows are falling out . . . the diocese won't do anything about it and there's no landlord to badger.

. . . or the people who maintained them:

> . . . the struggle we've had to get some work done on this house has been enormous because it was handled . . . by people who have no idea what it's

like to live in a [tied house]; it was very difficult to get them to see that a kitchen that's got walls falling down isn't ideal!

One person drew a contrast between their own house and the vicarage:

[The Vicar's wife] has talked to - - - and me about the comparative running costs of the house[s]. This house is very comfortable and efficient to run: the vicarage is a barn; their quarterly bills for fuel and electricity are the equivalent of our annual ones. If I get 'promotion' and become a vicar, I could be worse off very easily . . .

Another curate pointed to another problem with tied housing:

It has happened to me that any old person can waltz in and say, 'This is church property'. . . . When I was [away] the Archdeacon . . . came . . . [and] he'd taken the opportunity to look in every single room in the house. . . . I knew he was coming to look at the kitchen, but the churchwarden had shown him all round the house.

There were other consequences of working from home:

A problem we had as a family, which I don't think we ever got any help with, was people knocking on the door asking for money. . . . [The house is] back off the road, dark and secluded, and perhaps because we're on one of the main routes in and out of town we get a lot of people coming; people who smelled of glue, people who'd been in mental homes . . . a chap who was subsequently arrested by the police for a long-term con . . . and we felt very vulnerable; what happens if the children are in on their own, and so on. Yet at the same time we recognised there is an imperative to help the poor. . . . In the end we devised a strategy for dealing with it, which I don't think is ideal by any means, but everybody in the house knows what they have to do under certain circumstances.

Before leaving this part of the survey, it is worth drawing together some impressions from the interviews. On the whole, there was little sense that some of the restrictive expectations laid on clergy and their families in the past were experienced by the interviewees; particularly the ideas of a necessary aloofness, or 'apart-ness' from everyday society of the clergy as a group.[4] On the contrary, there was a strong expectation that clergy would be a part of the church communities in which they worked, often on first-name terms and terms of personal friendship with laypeople. This emphasis reflects much of the thinking about the nature of the local church over the past half-century, embodied in developments like the Parish Communion Movement and the new eucharistic liturgies which it has influenced. While the abandonment of many old assumptions was generally welcome, it could have unexpected difficulties. Several interviewees were married to partners who chose not to worship in the church in which the curate worked, sometimes because their religious affiliations were other than to the Anglican versions of Christianity: these people sometimes found an incomprehension among laypeople that their partners went elsewhere. Similarly, as in the comments about money, there was a failure to appreciate the difference between clergy, whose job was to work for the church, and laypeople who attended voluntarily; or that clergy might wish to support bodies other than their local church with time and money.

Some long-standing expectations were still operative; the clergy as dispensers of money to the poor; or as the ever-available patient listeners; or, interestingly in view of what was said earlier, as those whose lives were not really in tune with the concerns of the everyday world about money, career, sex, privacy, security; 'odd (wo)men out', curiosities, novelties. These expectations were tied up with people's perceptions, or fantasies, about the churches and could be both positive, attracting admiration and thanks, or negative, attracting stereotyping and marginalisation. Not surprisingly, many interviewees were keen to be seen both as credible clergy, but also credible human beings.

THE FUTURE

Curacies are, by their nature, time-bound appointments expected to last no more than four years and sometimes less. By the time they have reached the end curates are eligible to be appointed as incumbents in their own right; or they may choose to work in some other kind of ministry such as a hospital, university or prison chaplaincy, or in diocesan education, mission or social responsibility structures. There are no institutional barriers to Anglican clergy moving between dioceses in search of jobs, but considerations, many like those outlined in Chapter 2 as affecting first appointments, may incline clergy to remain in the diocese in which they have already worked, in which case they are much more dependent on their bishop's view of the direction of their future ministries.

Clearly linked to curates' expectations of the future are their understandings of what they are presently doing. Interviewees were asked what they thought the rationale of their present work was and whether they felt this understanding was one which others – those with whom they worked and the Church at large – might recognise. They were then asked what, given a totally free choice, they would like to do next; and whether they felt this was possible in reality.

All the interviewees' understandings of what they were doing fell within familiar and theologically well-supported categories; they spoke of their work as being the person who publicly represented God and the Church in a locality; as the enabler and encourager of the Church in a place; as the proclaimer of the Word of God, the administrator of the sacraments and the conductor of rites of passage; as the befriender or pastor to the poor, the sick and the needy. These understandings were, in general, felt to be shared by at least some of the people with whom they worked and by the wider Church. Several people drew parallels between their own experience and that of others as a way of discussing their ministries, as here:

> In the end I go back to Gospel stuff; I feel I'm doing what I want to be doing, I'm being myself quite fully. [I think of Jesus' saying] 'I have come that they may have life in all its fullness'; what I am, I'm helping others to be. . . . I want others to be in a position to [realise their potential], which is why all the social issues are so important.

These essentially modest understandings were reflected in people's hopes for the future. The great majority saw their work being within a parochial context, though a significant number felt they would like to try their hand at some other form of ministry, often some kind of institutional chaplaincy. One person expressed their hopes for:

> Interesting jobs, I think; that's all I want really, interesting and challenging jobs where I can bring skills from one area into another. It might be that there are some skills along the way that are never used, or might not be used for a long, long time; I'm not sure which way it'll go. . . . I might be a jobbing minister doing bits, the proverbial nought-point-five teacher, or point-two of this; some of it may be doing new things, or doing things that haven't been widely done.

Another person hoped to utilise their experience as a lay Christian:

> If you've been a lay person in a church [for a substantial period of time] . . . you know what it's like on the other side of the fence; you know how awkward and frustrating clergy can be. . . . I'm hoping I don't lose those insights and those lessons – I don't think I will . . . but I hope I can use some of them to help the laity develop [independence and self-confidence].

Given the general modesty of these expectations, it is interesting that a number of interviewees were not always very optimistic about the reality of future work. Several reflected the uncertainty of the Church of England's financial position:

> My feeling is that it's not absolutely certain there'll be jobs in the future; although I suppose I'm optimistic enough to think that God doesn't call people and then abandon them. . . . I enjoy parish work, but I can't help feeling it only taps a fraction of the skills I've got and I wonder whether there's some other combination of jobs which might suit me and which might be what all this is about. I don't anticipate any dramatic change in our finances; we've just got to do the best we can to manage.

Others indicated that the diocese in which they worked did not seem to be very helpful either:

> The lack of employment security that there is in the church at the moment [concerns me]; which goes with the lack of money; there's no savings to build up from your stipend, which is worrying. . . . I'm not sure how it's going to pan out. . . . [In this

diocese] we've been told we will be made redundant
if we haven't found a job at the end of my fourth
year [in this curacy]; that means no house as well
as no job.

Another commented:

> It seems to me that the diocese assumes that because
> I'm working here now I will continue to work for
> them . . . and that I can just be moved around like
> a pawn on the diocesan chessboard. . . . [The dio-
> cese] will simply move me around when it suits them.

While many people can see the deficiencies in their employers'
practices, there were some telling criticisms of the ways in
which appointments were handled in dioceses and in the
Church more generally:

> I don't necessarily think the Church has developed
> ways of discerning how to use talents which people
> have got . . . they tend . . . to put people into jobs
> because it's expedient to move them from A to B
> and not because they're suited to a particular job.
> That makes me angry because they . . . ought to be
> able to use the skills developed in other areas of
> life to apply [them] to the church. . . . People like
> bishops and incumbents are not familiar with the
> ways of modern interviewing techniques . . . they're
> much more comfortable with the personal, idiosyn-
> cratic way of dealing with things.

Again:

> I find the appointments system bizarre; you just
> don't know where the jobs are half the time so you
> haven't got an opportunity to say, 'Look, I could
> do that job and this is what I could bring to it.' . . .

> You don't know where the vacancies are because . . .
> there are at least half-a-dozen different sources of
> vacancies. They're not co-ordinated in any way
> and you can't necessarily find out what they are; I
> find that very strange coming from a different
> background. . . . I don't see the advantage of the
> secrecy . . . there's lots of vested interests who don't
> want to give up their say in making an appointment.

Such criticisms as these mirror the processes outlined in
Chapter 2 for finding curacies for ordinands; they are telling
in that they are made by people who often were responsible
for appointing and managing staff in their previous jobs. In
this they differ from most of the people making appointments
in the Church of England today since bishops and archdeacons,
as well as many incumbents, have generally spent the whole
of their careers within the Church and have never experienced
other ways of working; moreover, bishops and archdeacons
who have benefited personally by the present system may be
disinclined to criticise or change it. As will be discussed further
in Chapter 6, they may also have gained considerable power
from their ability to affect the workings of the present system
and this may be another disincentive to change practice.
There is an ideological aspect to this: far too many clergy are
inclined to assume that the way things are currently managed
is an essential consequence of priestly, or episcopal, authority.
There is frequently little awareness that bishops and other
clergy can, and do, work with much more participative and
democratic structures than are generally found in the Church
of England without loss of Christian authority; in the churches
as elsewhere, it is necessary to pose questions about power,
vested interest and resistance to change. People with different
experiences found their skills undervalued:

> I think one of the things I've been particularly good
> at has been . . . building teams and getting people

to work together . . . [but] I haven't really got the church experience to put me in that position. I need to persuade people that these skills are as important as the church experience . . . [Having the requisite number of years in the Church] is how bishops got to be bishops.

A woman echoed the latter point from her experience of applying for a job:

The reason I didn't get the job wasn't because I didn't have the right qualifications . . . but because I hadn't been ordained long enough. . . . The criteria involved in choosing the person were not necessarily related to the talents you might think you'd have to have for a particular job. . . . On that showing I'll still be here in fifty years' time; there are [*n*] women being ordained [priest] in [this] diocese soon, many of whom are years senior to me . . . I don't find that very acceptable.

Several people were prepared to contemplate working in non-stipendiary ministry for a part of their careers, particularly if this would enable them to pursue particular emphases in ministry. There was a sense that this might not always be received sympathetically, however:

It's not really approved of in this diocese, non-stipendiary ministry . . . [The diocese] is very conservative . . . locked into this model of ministry as being the parish church; that's where the Church's ministry and mission take place. Every time we have a discussion about finance and mission and ministry it all comes back to the idea that this all happens in the parishes and everything else is just a burden on the parishes financially. . . . I find

most clergy are very happy with this model of parish
ministry, with themselves as kings of the castle. . . .
They just don't understand [any alternative].

VIEWS OF THE CHURCH

As a means of testing their comments about future work,
interviewees were asked how their attitude towards the Church
had developed since ordination; how similar was it to what they
had thought and felt as students? In view of the comments
made above about the ways the Church was perceived through
the appointments process, most people were surprisingly
positive. However, it became clear as they spoke that many
people most valued the local Church, including the one where
they worked, and sometimes a conception of the universal
Church; but they generally were sceptical, or critical, of the
Church at diocesan or denominational level. Several people
admitted that they tried to consider the Church primarily as
a worshipping community rather than an organisational structure, since the latter context was the one in which it appeared
at its least impressive. This adjustment of personal perspective
is interesting, not least because it can shut out a wide-ranging
discussion about the organisation with which ministers' identi-
ties are closely bound up and about which there is often very
little theological material or conceptual language. We will
return to this question in Chapter 6, but for the moment here
are several comments which largely speak for themselves.
One comment reflects the division between attitudes to the
local and the national aspects noted above:

> I'm very proud to be Anglican . . . I wasn't born
> and bred with it and take it for granted and . . . up
> to a point I won't have it knocked; I don't think
> the grass is greener on the other side because I
> know it's not. . . . [but] The leadership make me
> very angry sometimes; that they can appoint David

Hope as Archbishop when he's against the ordination of women – that is absolutely intolerable. How women must feel about that, heaven only knows. . . . I hate deanery synods and things like that – just appalling! The bureaucracy and hierarchy of it, I'm not in love with that. But the local church, I love it to death . . . that's not because I happen to work here; I'm proud of our local church, but the hierarchy and bureaucracy does get to me; and the public school image of it all.

Several people felt that although they had no personal experience of being poorly treated, others had not been so fortunate:

[The Church] has left me alone [but] I have observed . . . that people who fall foul of it are treated in strange ways . . . which when you look at them aren't the sorts of thing you'd expect from a caring organisation. . . . [It] has got a lot to learn about how to treat people. . . . We seem to be in a medieval bureaucracy which churns away and chews people up. Those aspects of the church I don't like; we're slightly hypocritical on that one. . . . [But] it's all right if you don't rock the boat.

Again:

[I'm surprised at] the appointments system and the way clergy are handled. I know that certain clergy, not necessarily in this diocese . . . who struggled weren't helped terribly well, and it can seem a very unchristian structure. I think it's fortunate that the experience I've had in this diocese has been completely the other way.

Another person identified a major structural problem . . .

I think it's very sexist. . . . In this diocese the senior
staff consists of a group of fifteen people, which is
quite a large number, and they make all the . . . key
decisions . . . they're all men and they're not open
to having a woman on that [group] unless and until
a woman is an archdeacon at the very least. So
appointments which involve women . . . have no
woman having any say in that [process]. . . . In that
respect I think there's scant attention paid to particular problems to do with women and the deploy-
ment of women. [The church] purports to be
democratic . . . but in reality the power is kept in
the hands of a very small number of people and it's
quite difficult to get information, or to get beyond
the bishop saying, 'Well, I'll think about it.'

. . . while another commented:

There's the careerism and the slippery pole which
is being climbed and the sort of things which I
hear colleagues talking about – I was quite shocked
by it, really. . . . People say, 'If you want to do this,
you should go and do this and you should know
that person . . . you should get yourself involved in
this committee.' . . . People say to me, 'Do you
have any contacts?' – but you are aware that people
do have contacts and they *do* know bishops and
archdeacons . . . this is the way they see themselves
progressing. . . . I'm aware very much how influence and gossip affects an awful lot: and rumour;
you know, 'the rumour is that he's moving because
. . .'. You realise they're also talking about you; I
met someone who said they knew all about me and
I thought, 'How? I've never met you before; how
have you heard about me?'

Finally in this chapter, one interviewee made a plea for greater understanding of curates' experiences of ministry, which reflects much that was said in the course of all these conversations:

> I think that curates do need a lot more support: I think people underestimate the feelings of insecurity, certainly re the next post. It's all very well saying you don't care about the future, but there is a point where you do very much care where the next job's going to come from. There should be a lot more affirming of what you've done; I've gone through three years of no one actually telling me. You don't do it for congratulations, but it actually would be quite nice for someone to say, 'You're all right, you are actually doing your job.'

NOTES

1 In 1995 there were 376 such dignitaries out of 10,260 stipendiary clergy in the Church of England. Source: *The Church of England Year Book 1997*, Church House Publishing (1997), p. 180.

2 George Orwell, *A Clergyman's Daughter*, Victor Gollancz (1935).

3 Text in Alan Bennett, 'Bed Among the Lentils' in *Talking Heads*, London, BBC Books (1988), pp. 29-41, and Joanna Trollope, *The Rector's Wife*, London, Bloomsbury Publishing (1991).

4 For a discussion of the development of this ideal, see Anthony Russell, *The Clerical Profession*, London, SPCK (1980), pp. 235 ff.

CHAPTER 6

What is happening and what can be done?

Is ministry in the Church of England a chaplaincy to society, or should it be saying something about the way society should be living? Are we involved in reformist social work, rather than saying that something is wrong and we should kick it out? . . . There are lots of these tensions, and it's stuff that there's never an answer on, but you continue to struggle with it, trying to push it a bit further.

RECAPITULATION

This chapter offers some analysis of the material presented so far and attempts to set the interviewees' experiences into some kind of context. But first let's review the main points which arise from my conversations with curates.

The most fundamental difficulty, reported by the majority of those interviewed, was that they had no effective working relationship with their training incumbents. In many cases this was as basic as having no time together to discuss what they had been doing, how they expected their work to develop and to plan ahead for the immediate future. Larger-scale projects, like a training plan for the curacy, or reflecting on experience as an integral part of a learning process, were in most cases non-existent and so improbable that, when asked about them, most curates simply laughed. The unavoidable conclusion to be drawn from these realities alone is that the majority of the curates had received no training at the start of their ordained ministries and that their training incumbents were so in name only.

The most common explanation for this lack of working and training structure was that training incumbents were over-busy and lacked the personal organisational skills to make time for discussion and training. Such an analysis locates problems with curacies in an essentially practical context and suggests that the solution may lie in encouraging clergy to be less busy and to learn the necessary management skills to make them more effective. This is a straightforward, functional response which appeals to directors of clergy training and others; but may need to be treated with scepticism because it avoids many of the questions about why clergy work as they do. In any event, the fact that a minority of curates believed they had received a useful training from their incumbents indicates not only that some clergy can find time to train others but also that attitude plays a significant part.

There was evidence that the ways in which curates were found jobs, and even the jobs themselves, left much to be desired. Far too little attention was paid to how the curate was to be trained, beyond vague and well-meaning generalisations, something as true of the diocesan training plans as the incumbents who were responsible for implementing them. The lack of a proper interviewing procedure and virtually non-existent monitoring at all levels compounded the vagueness, which was also matched by the selection of training incumbents. As noted in Chapter 2, the criteria for selection were indeterminate and generalised, and no training was required before a decision was taken to offer an incumbent a curate. Subsequent training and, even more important, monitoring of the training offered, were weak. But this is not to accuse bishops, DDOs and directors of POT of total ignorance about incumbents' abilities, since cases were also reported of them knowing about problems, or disasters, with past curates, even though this did not prevent further curates from being sent to work with the clergy concerned. This highlights questions about the assumptions which underlie bishops' policies on appointments, a matter which cannot simply be addressed by better training.

On the other hand, the curates interviewed were generally positive about their dealings with other clergy, authorised ministers like Readers, and with lay people, both within and beyond the churches' regular membership. Although they often expressed criticisms of the Church and doubts about themselves, there was little sense that they disliked the work they were doing or felt that they had been fundamentally mistaken in pursuing their sense of vocation. They also showed a degree of adaptability in thinking about what they might do in the future in a Church which was changing and where past assumptions about jobs might not apply. By the end of the interviews it was clear that those selected would prove to be reliable witnesses of the realities of ministry, hardly people so beset by personal difficulties and failings that their problems were more likely to be of their own making than reflections of the system in which they worked. The only surprise was that so many had experienced such difficulties in their early years and that their experiences seemed to have so many common factors, despite differences of geography, temperament and family circumstances. All this suggests that the matters raised here have a far wider significance than simply training curates.

SOME PRELIMINARY INTERPRETATIONS

There are a number of possible reactions to, or interpretations of, the material from these interviews, which may be summarised as follows.

'What have curates got to worry about?'

Curates, like other clergy, may think they have problems, but these are nothing compared with other people. The churches have not experienced the traumatic restructuring of other organisations in the last two decades. Clergy are very unlikely to be made redundant, spend long periods of time unemployed, or find that by 45 they are considered too old for future work. They have a house with the job which is often larger and more expensive than they, or many of their parishioners, could afford for themselves, and a non-contributory pension on retirement. Even if their income is modest this is more than compensated for by a far greater personal freedom to work as they wish. There is little close supervision, no restrictive code of practice, and only a token appraisal process compared with most other jobs. Surveys frequently indicate that clergy enjoy higher job satisfaction and lower occupational stress levels than other comparable workers. In any event, they have consciously chosen this way of life and even today enjoy a higher social status and esteem than most other people. Any complaints are of little significance compared with what other people experience every day in the struggle to make ends meet.

'It's only for a few years'

On this view curates' complaints about their initial experiences in ministry are about relatively transitory matters. This might reflect the episcopal view that they can be 'licked into shape' – whatever that might mean – or else that, provided they can weather the problems of the curacy for three or four years, they will eventually be offered an incumbency of their own. There they will either have a free hand to do as they wish – or come to realise that their training incumbents' attitudes were right all along and eventually they will think and act in the same way. They may even come to be grateful for what happened to them as curates, recognising it as character-forming.

'This can be resolved by a new training programme'

In the period since starting this research in 1994 I have discussed my findings with a number of people, including those involved in POT and other clergy in-service training. The widespread recognition within this constituency of the reality of the problems identified is often accompanied by the view that the application of suitable training programmes would eliminate, or at least significantly reduce, the nature of the problem. One or two people I met expressed the view that the new training programme in the diocese of X would not only deal with the problem but prove so effective that it would be consigned to the dustbin of history. A parallel view was that, with more careful selection and training, a new generation of training incumbents would emerge who would avoid the mistakes of their predecessors.

All three of these perspectives contain a degree of truth, and it would be foolish to ignore some of their insights. All the curates I interviewed were aware of the very favourable position they enjoyed as clergy in relation to people in other occupations, including those in which they had previously worked. It was also true that in time the curates could expect to become incumbents and a number of the interviewees have already done so. It is reasonable to expect that in the future some will have curates of their own and it will be interesting to see how they use the insights gained from their own curacies. Given the long-standing nature of the problems identified it is entirely possible that some of the interviewees' training incumbents had themselves experienced similar problems in their own curacies. It is also true that better and more extensive training can influence people to adopt better working practices and become more effective, and that new training programmes can, indeed must, build on the experience of the past, good and bad.

Even so, these perspectives in themselves offer little hope that the problems identified in this research can be successfully addressed, much less eliminated. To stress the favourable position of clergy to someone experiencing the problems described by some interviewees is a *non sequitur*. To live in a pleasant house and to have job security does not address the sense that a person's integrity is compromised either by the work, or by their colleagues' attitudes; or the fear that they have made a fundamental mistake in being ordained, a mistake inflicted upon marital partner and children alike. The essential weakness of this argument is that it fails to address the vocational nature of ministry which demands a high level of personal integrity. This can best be demonstrated by turning the points on their heads; no clergy would be admired for basing their commitment to the job on the housing provided, job security, or freedom from supervision. To do so would invite the criticism that they were insincere timeservers, lacking in the dedication which ought to be the hallmark of ministry.

It is also true that curacies are only for a limited period of time. Once they are ended there will be ample opportunity for doing ministry one's own way. Anecdotal evidence suggests that many clergy have thought this way and still do; but it presupposes a way of working and an attitude to the task which is increasingly at variance with the realities of church life. There is general advocacy of a pattern of working involving partnership with others, rather than seeing the minister as an heroic individualist. This pattern takes as its theological justification the view that ministry must be part of the life of the whole Church, not simply an adjunct to it. Quite simply the individualist approach to ministry is often bad practice. Moreover, an observation from the interviews was that those who had experienced the greatest problems as curates were precisely the ones who were least interested in working in teams or groups in the future. There was a strong feeling that they were unwilling to be blocked or obstructed as they had been before. Bad experience as a curate may well promote bad practice as an incumbent, if only for lack of a good model of ministerial practice.

All these considerations impinge on training and shape the expectations which can be entertained of it. Much of the in-service training offered in the churches is based on an essentially liberal/rational view which sees people as generally open to new insights, able to recognise good when they see it and willing to change in response. It is important to identify this as an ideological perspective, rather than treat it as an objective truth. It has certain strengths, but it runs into difficulties when applied to people whose motivations are more complex, or simply different. In the case of clergy it does not allow for the power of prior ideological commitments to certain interpretations of vocation; or of the power of external expectations, habit and established routine; or of simple unwillingness or inability to reflect on what one is doing, or imagine other ways of working. From personal experience the least satisfactory training incumbents are often those least willing to attend any training event; they either flatly refuse, or else agree, only to withdraw at the last moment because of an unexpected funeral.

A further criticism of these perspectives is that they all fail to locate any responsibility for change with those who oversee and operate the levers of power and the process of appointments. While it would be foolish to lay all the responsibility at the doors of bishops and DDOs, there seems to be a pressing need for a radical reform of this process, not only because it would benefit curates but also because it would help to re-cast the Church's assumptions of how ministry is undertaken. In Chapter 4 it was argued that POT, and other in-service training in the Church, was hampered by a lack of organisational working objectives, which in other occupations form the basis of staff training and development. We now consider this further.

SURVIVAL: AN INDUSTRIAL PARABLE

It is now widely recognised that the churches in Britain are often engaged in a struggle for institutional survival. The preeminence they enjoyed in the past has been severely eroded by falling numbers, indifference to religious observance, shortages of money and clergy, and ageing congregations. To set this ecclesiastical discussion in some wider context we look now at another example of a survival strategy.

In May 1997 I visited Tinsley Bridge Ltd, a small specialised steelworks in Sheffield producing suspension components for the automotive industry. The firm, whose origins go back to the nineteenth century when it produced springs and other components for the railways, was part of British Steel prior to its privatisation, when it was transformed into a small, independent producer through a management buy-out. Supplying automotive components is a very competitive business, working to demanding specifications and very precise delivery schedules in a market which is constantly changing with the introduction of new models and where fluctuations in international exchange rates can transform profit into loss overnight. To survive in such a market, Tinsley Bridge had to adapt and change continually. There had been redundancies and across-the-board reductions in pay in order that the firm as a whole could remain viable. There had also had to be major changes in the work culture which affected all employees. The men on the shop floor, who handled the heavy steel billets, sometimes heated to 900° centigrade, in and out of hydraulic presses which shaped and prepared them for machining and finishing, were organised in teams, each with a team leader. A great deal of responsibility had been devolved onto workers with a relatively modest formal education, who realised that a significant part of the firm's viability, and with it their own jobs and those of their colleagues, were in their hands. The culture of co-operation, shared decision-making and collective responsibility was much spoken about and, I guessed, a reality in a way it could not have been in the past. This had necessitated changes in everyone's attitudes, managers as well as shop-floor workers, and gave a new emphasis to training, which was seen as an essential tool in helping people adapt, change and survive in a city badly hit by unemployment and the decline of traditional heavy industry.

Stories like this inevitably have a range of potential interpretations and understandings. Why should people have to work in this pressured, highly competitive capitalist structure? What about those made redundant so that the firm could survive? Is the implicit threat of further redundancy a goad to pressure people into accepting the unacceptable? How far was all this talk of teamwork and co-operation merely a smokescreen camouflaging old divisions between bosses and workers? But while recognising the force and urgency of these questions, I remained impressed by the sense in which Tinsley Bridge's survival strategy, and no doubt that of countless other similar firms, was worlds away from what still passes for normal in the churches and among clergy. Whatever larger questions there might be, the shop-floor workers who sweated and manhandled the hot steel into the presses day after day *did* work as a team; they *did* have a sense of solidarity and common interest; they *did* realise that they simply could not expect to go on as they had done before. Examining what was done and how, thinking of how it might be improved, learning from mistakes and building on good practice *was* a reality and they knew it could not be treated just as an option for those who liked that sort of thing. But this process, unlike much in-service training in the churches, was based on short- and medium-term working objectives, rather than wide, over-arching long-term aims. Workers were not simply exhorted in general terms to work together and promote the prosperity of the company; these aims were translated into specific objectives which could be embodied into training programmes, learned and assessed. Moreover, the outcomes of the learning, and people's ability to translate it into practice, was an integral consideration in people's career development.[1]

THE IMPORTANCE OF NOT BEING RICHARD

The counterpoint to this story from Sheffield is provided by Charles Handy, himself a lay Christian and a critical supporter of the churches:

> 'Well, at least that's one book I won't have to read,' said Richard, laughing, when I told him that I was writing a book about getting organised. Richard is our local vicar.

'Why not?' I said, just slightly offended.

'Well, it's for managers, isn't it – businessmen, that sort of people?'

'It's not only for them,' I said, 'it's for everyone who has responsibility for other people or who needs to get things done by other people. And that must include you, Richard,' I added.

'Oh, I'm not much good at that sort of thing,' he said, 'getting people to do things.'[2]

Richard appears to speak for many clergy; concepts like organisation, management and team-working are not really for him. They belong to the world of other people's work and he is not in the least abashed to admit his ignorance of them, while his cheery dismissal, 'That's one book I won't have to read', suggests that he sees no reason to rectify the situation. Training for Richard is simply not an issue because there is nothing to learn, even though if he were questioned further he would be at pains to emphasise that his work is with and for people; even that it was 'people-centred'. He might seek to justify his unwillingness to think or read about organisation on the grounds that he preferred to be dealing with people – 'what I was ordained for'. The liberal/rational view of education depends on curiosity or a belief that there may be other ways of working which are worth hearing about; without these there is no starting-point for exploration. This is recognised in industrial and professional training outside the churches where another element is introduced; unless workers continually update their skills and learn ways of working in line with the employer's policy and objectives, they risk becoming unemployable or seeing their workplace close. One major difference between Tinsley Bridge and the Church of England is that at the steelworks the employees knew this, even if they accepted it grudgingly, whereas in the Church this mostly goes unrecognised in a pervasive culture of *laissez-faire*.

Richard may well be an example of the heroic individualism so beloved of generations of clergy; related to Jeffrey Cox's 'Civilising Mission of the Churches'.[3] It appears that this way of thinking and working lies behind the problems which many of the interviewees' training incumbents created for them. These clergy work alone for much of the time, in the sense that they constantly deal with people and situations as lone operators; they see a person who is sick, visit a bereaved family, conduct a service or take a school assembly. They give, others receive. Their work is not only fragmented temporally, with lots of short items one after another; it is also atomised, with lots of individual contacts, conversations and outputs. In some cases this may seem to be an inevitable consequence of the job; but there may also be cases where in so dealing with individuals, clergy effectively prevent those people interacting with each other and so forming ideas or expressing opinions which may be at variance with the minister's. This is not fanciful; I was told several years ago of a clergyman who, anxious that the church council should not vote against him on a matter, went round to each of them individually before the meeting to persuade them to do what he wanted.[4] Behind this seems to lie attitudes suspicious of laypeople, seeing them as potential rivals, or worse, a theme reflected not only by the interviewees' comments on their colleagues' ideas about leadership, quoted in Chapter 4, but also many 'clerical manuals', books written about ministry by clergy for clergy.[5]

But surely clergy are part of the Church and relate to the congregation in the parish as a basic part of their work? Has not the sense that the liturgical assembly, primarily in the act of celebrating Holy Communion together, developed a greater sense of its corporate identity in this century through the Parish Communion Movement[6] than hitherto? Indeed: but this does not appear to have substantially undermined their heroic individualism. Despite the popularity of housegroups in many churches, the local church as a whole still only really gathers together for worship on Sundays; such worship in almost all the mainstream denominations still relies heavily on the pattern of one person at the front conducting what goes on, speaking, preaching, proclaiming, exhorting, directing. Worship is rarely a shared, discursive experience in which people relate directly to one another to discuss the scriptures, consider subjects for prayer, speak about experiences, hopes or fears, and try to discern the hand of God. Moreover, in the Church of England the focal liturgical figure is most often one who is ordained. So too with pastoral care, where much that is offered is focused on a liturgical act of baptism, wedding or funeral: in the dramatic sense, this is performance as pastoral care. As with individual contacts, so in liturgy, clergy act as givers to receivers, leaders to followers, informed to uninformed. There is little sense that they work with, and within, a group where people are seen more as equals, each with something to contribute and each with something to learn. This point was expressed and expounded by interviewees:

> The Church disempowers people all the time; it's all about saying, 'You can't do this and you can't do that', both in the way it conducts itself when it meets together in liturgy, full of rules about what you can and can't do, and in terms of the whole thing about Christian morality; it's very much rule-based and the message people get from the Church all the time is, 'Thou shalt not . . .' . . . so that's one reason why I feel very uncomfortable with the Church because what I want to be about as a person is empowering people, both as individuals to be themselves and within the institutions which they're part of, convincing them they have some power to change things: it's *very* hard work in the Church, encouraging people to think things like that!

Again:

The whole thing about the hierarchical structure where we have professional priesthood at the top who 'do' ministry and the rest who are receivers of ministry just doesn't mean very much in today's world; some of the best responses I had from people in my last parish was where we tried to overturn that and actually look at – it's a cliché, I know – 'every member ministry'; that everybody has some-thing to contribute. . . . In the church that I'm in now, people regard it as a place of safety; quite a few of them have come from other churches where they've had changes in the liturgy or church building, or whatever, and they've escaped; they've come [here] and they thought it was a safe haven where nothing was ever going to change.

There is another aspect which bears on this research. The Parish Communion Movement emphasised the offering by the eucharistic assembly of the whole of life as Christian people in the world. This implicitly meant that the world of work was to be understood as a locus of Christian discipleship in the fullest sense and that what was said, done and experienced there was of fundamental concern to the Christian assembly when it gathered, 'for the Lord's service around the Lord's table on the Lord's Day'. Here too, unfortunately, there seems little sense that clergy are effective, or even interested. A survey produced several years ago questioned almost 400 women and men from all the major Christian denominations about the ways in which they saw their work as an integral part of their Christian discipleship; the degree of recognition of this by the churches to which they belonged; and the extent of the encouragement, interest and support which the Church, including its ministers, offered to them.

About half . . . found their minister to be of little or no help in this context. But about a third found

> clerical support [sometimes from a chaplain who
> was not their local priest] valuable, the key feature
> again being a genuine interest in their working
> lives and a readiness to listen and learn.[7]

This statement is virtually interchangeable with the comments
made by the curates in this survey. It is this parallelism which
underlines why what happens to curates in the early years of
ministry is important to the churches, since it both reflects
the disinterest which clergy seem to have in the world of work
– anyone's work – as a consequence of their professional
individualism. It also suggests that the ideal of clergy as
'enablers' of others rather than 'do-ers' of ministry, as
encouragers and partners of other people's discipleship, is
critically undermined by the current church culture. This
may be because in the churches the concept of Christians at
work is effectively inverted; able-bodied laypeople are there
to support the clergy, rather than *vice versa*, and only qualify
for support themselves when they fall ill, or are bereaved, or
in some kind of distress. This idea that the clergy are the ones
who 'do' ministry gains support from official documents.
The Synodical Government Measure of 1969 states:

> [2] The functions of parochial church councils shall
> include –
> [a] co-operation with the incumbent in promoting
> in the parish the whole mission of the Church,
> pastoral, evangelistic, social and ecumenical.[8]

While this wording could imply that 'the whole mission of
the Church' is shared between incumbent and laypeople, the
clergy's focal role in so much of a congregation's life leans
heavily towards the view that this is the incumbent's job, in
which s/he is supported and assisted by laypeople.

Clergy are therefore carers for those in distress; but care
can have ideological consequences, as an interviewee observed:

> I think the Church as an employing organisation leaves a great deal to be desired. . . . In some ways it looks after people; to put the positive things, there's provision for people in need of a rest, or for people having breakdowns, or families needing to go on holiday, or to educate their children away from home . . . In some ways it's quite generous in looking after its members, but I think in terms of actually providing a proper support system it's very bad.

This culture of caring justifies an individualistic approach on the grounds that problems are individualised. It also disarms criticism: who would be churlish enough to criticise the vicar or the bishop when he was so kind and helpful over a personal crisis, or a bereavement, or an illness? In this context it is significant that many interviewees made favourable comments about the support they thought they might expect, or had received, from senior diocesan staff. But whether or not they realise it, this pastoral care has a political and power aspect – it oils the wheels of a machine which it might be better to modify, or replace altogether.[9] There is also the possibility of a care system doubling as a means of control: not to offer care is also an option, people can be left to sink or swim when in trouble and the possibility of this may be a powerful disincentive to complain or be difficult.[10]

Finally, curates are, for many training incumbents, a status symbol, a sign of episcopal favour, maybe even a foretaste of better things to come. In other words, curates are not ends in themselves, as much Christian theology insists persons must be, but means to other ends. It has already been noted that bishops and DDOs are frequently reluctant to refuse to give a curate to a senior incumbent in a diocese: this is a part of a process of patronage which depends not upon a person's abilities or skills in ministry, but upon long service, loyalty to the diocesan organisation, perhaps a willingness in the past to undertake a difficult or unpopular task. Patronage is about cultivating a favourable group of supporters, or having the potential to reward others' compliance or loyalty. It is a system of calculation, of weighing personal benefit, of reciprocal favours and bargaining for advantage. This is all too often the system which operates in dioceses in the Church of England and it is diametrically opposed to a culture of advancement by merit. As one interviewee noted, the likelihood of being offered a particular job in the church is usually a product of a person's years in ordained ministry; the less years, the less prestigious the job, even if a person has a clutch of well-developed skills which might be beneficial. The prestigious jobs, in large, well-funded parishes go to those who have completed sufficient years in ministry, even though such churches may demand less ministerial skill to run than the small, poorly resourced churches in inner-city or rural areas which are frequently offered to curates at the end of curacies. This too is a powerful disincentive to a culture of job-related learning; why spend time learning and developing skills when no one pays them any heed in considering future work?

THE CULTURE OF HEROIC INDIVIDUALISM

On the basis of this analysis, it is not difficult to see why curates are so often effectively abandoned by their training incumbents almost from the outset of their ministries. The culture of individualism does not presuppose any real working together at the tasks of ministry because they are individual, personal, confidential. Anything which takes the minister away from these tasks, which compromises their availability to others, is to be avoided. Curates need to realise this as soon as possible; but such a release to 'do their own thing' may, on this understanding, be a kind of affirmation, conveying the same freedom as the incumbent enjoys. Of course, there are potential problems, particularly if the curate and incumbent cannot avoid working at the same task, or with the same group of people. Here, care must be taken to avoid the curate interfering with the incumbent's freedom of action, or upstaging him, even if unintentionally. Recourse can here be made to the hierarchical pattern of organisation still enshrined in much of the Church's assumptions about ministry. Years in ministry can be used to bolster authority, even if this pays scant regard for actual skills and talents. Similarly, curates, like laypeople, must be seen to be loyal to their incumbents, to support them publicly, to avoid rocking the boat.

In such a situation training is hardly a major consideration. People do as they see fit, no doubt guided by some inner sense of duty and conviction. Their good deeds, their simple care of others in need, will more than justify what they do and may earn enough gratitude or respect to stand the minister in good stead if from time to time they make mistakes. Reflection on practice, the possibility of learning from success or failure, is, like the rest of ministry, a purely personal matter; though there is always the possibility that in reality many people do not reflect at all. The idea that reflection might be done collectively with colleagues is more than outweighed, as one interviewee suggested, by the possibility that this might lead to confrontation or dispute. There is, in any event, no real need to monitor training because as long as curates complete their four years of curacy without any significant problems, they will in all probability be offered another job in the diocese. Unless there has been a very public failure on their part, no one has sufficient evidence on which to judge the matter anyway.

The extent of such practice in the Church of England seems amply demonstrated by events which made the headlines in 1995. In August of that year the news broke that a curate in Sheffield, the Reverend Chris Brain, had been accused of misconduct, including improper sexual relationships, within a new experimental congregation known as the Nine O'clock Service (NOS), an attempt to devise a form of worship and church which drew heavily on rock culture, ecology and post-modern ideas. As the reports grew ever more lurid NOS was described as a 'rave' church, or a 'cult', and Brain emerged as a highly skilled manipulator of literally dozens of the congregation's key members whom he succeeded in charming and bullying over a period of years. Eventually Brain resigned and the debacle disappeared from public view.[11] What seemed incredible at the time and since is that at virtually no point was Brain, a layperson when NOS first began, subject to any close or systematic supervision from the vicar of the church in which it was launched, or from the senior staff of the diocese, even though NOS was widely regarded as a vitally important evangelistic initiative for the Church of England as a whole, and tangible evidence of its resolve to address contemporary culture. Perhaps the apparent success of the service seemed to place its organisation and practice beyond questioning: but it was precisely this lack of oversight which gave Brain all the opportunity he needed to establish his domination over others. It also emerged that a member of NOS had gone to the bishop with allegations of Brain's misdemeanours, but no action was taken because she was thought to be an unreliable witness. While the story of the Nine O'clock Service has many other implications for the churches, it is clear in this context that the unwillingness of training incumbents to supervise their curates has parallels at the highest levels.[12]

CAN ANYTHING BE DONE?

In 1961 the then Bishop of Southwell, Frank Russell Barry, wrote:

> If we have fewer men, they will have to be far better trained and qualified: for everybody will have to count for more than one. . . . The ordained ministry must be envisaged in the only context in which it makes sense – within the total ministry of the Church

as the Body of Christ in the world. The clergy in future will have to be leaders and overseers of this corporate and mainly lay leadership. That is going to give them a new status and rescue them from being 'odd men out'. But this again means that they must be better trained. The evocation and nurturing of lay ministries will depend on the quality of the ordained ministry. If the latter is weak the former will not be there, and the Church will become more clerical than ever.[13]

Even in 1961 this was no new idea. It had been widely canvassed in the period since 1945 and it was certainly being advocated in 1920.[14] But many of the findings of this research confirm that little progress has been made towards this pattern of ministry in the intervening years. This may be because too little attention has been paid to the structural and procedural changes which would be required to make it a reality; there is often a pious hope that external influences – falling numbers of clergy, shortages of money, a more educated laity, greater social marginalisation of the churches – will somehow effect the desired results without the churches having to take any hard decisions themselves.

But it may also be because of a widespread reluctance to question assumptions about vocation and long-standing patterns of ministerial practice. Much lip-service has been paid to a ministry of 'enabling', or partnership, or collaboration; but all too often this has dissolved at the first sign of difficulty and recourse made to the old ways. There has been an assumption that *of course* clergy will carry on with their individualistic ways of working, keeping ministry to themselves, or at least safely behind church doors, because realistically that is the only way it can be. It is easy to see why. This is the culture in which so many clergy, including bishops, have grown up and worked; it is familiar territory and, if things get difficult, there is much comfort to be had from staying with the known, rather than branching out into the unknown. Besides, new ways take time, demand new skills, threaten the possibility of admitting that one is wrong, or ignorant; which in turn can be interpreted as weakness. Old ways are hallowed by precedent and by theology, even if sometimes the theology is suspect; new ways need new understandings and this too is hard and time-consuming. And time, as clergy keep repeating, is something they do not have: they are busy people, pressured by expectations, driven by a sense of duty, needing to justify themselves and God by activity, doing good, being with people. Better to get on with things rather than gaze at their navels to no good purpose. But there is also the sense that individualistic ways of working are more straightforward; it is easier to apportion blame when things go wrong or claim credit for success. Working with others spoils the simplicity of this arrangement, makes too many hostages to fortune, raises the need for negotiation, collective decision-making, shared leadership, conflict management; often precisely the areas clergy feel uncertain or fearful about.

The area of training curates may seem a very insignificant place to start, but I contend that an attempt to address the wider issues of the culture and assumptions about ministry will benefit a far wider constituency than junior clergy. Structural change is necessary because curates' difficulties are a symptom of something far more profound than poor relationships with an over-busy incumbent. The Church's central institutions and staff must be seen to be supporting and promoting the changes and willing to support objectives with resources of persons and training. Andrew Bowden has observed in connection with changing structures for ministry that three things are necessary:

> First, the diocese has to encourage initiatives and help set them up. Secondly, the clergy involved have to want to set them up. Thirdly, parishes and individuals need to be presented with a clear job specification of what they are being asked to do and

what training will be involved. It is not that laypeople are unwilling, but they would not dream of flying in the face of diocesan or clerical opposition: nor are they prepared, as it were, to sign a blank cheque.[15]

It is impossible, and undesirable, to suggest a complete, self-enclosed programme; change in one area will almost certainly have unforeseen consequences in others. What will be necessary is a willingness to keep reviewing and evaluating what is happening and seizing opportunities as they arise. What follows is an outline of ways to start the process.

1. Be clear about what is expected

Mention has been made in the course of this research of the vagueness which so frequently besets the training process for curates. It is essential that dioceses be clear about what is expected of all involved in training, including the nature and level of skills required for training incumbents, the time to be given to training and the frequency of training elements, and the processes of monitoring and evaluation. It is also important to be clear about the levels of competence required of curates as they proceed through the training process and what competences are needed for them to be eligible for a further appointment.

Behind this proposal is the pressing need for dioceses, and the Church as a whole, to be clear about what kinds of competences are required of those in ministry, at what level and when these competences need to be acquired in the course of a ministerial career. There must also be a parallel willingness to use these expectations in making decisions about appointments.

A necessary concomitant of this provision is that past experience and skills acquired before ordination must be properly recognised and taken into account as part of the training and appointment process.

2. Make the initial appointments process open

It is essential that the present system of appointing people to first curacies be abolished and replaced by one in which parishes, in partnership with the diocese, draw up a proper job description for curacies on the basis of which ordinands can apply for posts and be selected by competitive interview. The interviews should be conducted by a properly trained panel which includes the incumbent, a lay person from the congregation and a nominee of the bishop. Ordinands may apply for more than one post simultaneously. Reports on ordinands from the theological college or course should be made available to the interview panel. To ensure effective choice, there should be more posts available in any year than ordinands.

3. Parishes must assess their discipleship in relation to their context

This provision recognises the popularity of mission (or social) audits of congregations, as a tool to focus attention on opportunities for discipleship. They can, however, become simply a process of identifying openings into which the local church, its theology and ideas intact and unchanging, can make forays to recruit more members to its services.

The real importance of this contextual interest is to recognise the existing discipleship, commitment and theology not only of church members, but 'all people of good will' who together can work for the values enshrined in the Christian theme of 'the Kingdom of God'. This involves a major shift of emphasis away from the agendas of a clerical leadership towards a recognition that it is laypeople who are in the forefront of the mission of the Church and their insights and experience need to be valued as a primary foundation for the Church's theology and action.

It is also that proper official use needs to be made of the findings, as indicated below.

4. This analysis must form the basis for objectives for action, allocation of diocesan resources, including staff, and training

The audit process mentioned in 3 above should be used as the basis for a congregational development programme, covering up to five years from the point of production, of which possibly only the first two are outlined in detail. This programme will then form the basis for what is done in and by the congregation and will be used by the diocese, in consultation with the parish, to determine what staff may be appointed, as well as training to be offered for clergy and laypeople. No staff would be appointed by the diocese, or licensed by the bishop, without reference to the development programme. Job descriptions for such staff, including curates and their training incumbents, would be based on the information contained in the audit and the programme.

5. Parishes as a whole are periodically appraised on the basis of their self-defined objectives

The development programme would also contain the criteria against which the programme as a whole, the congregation and the staff, would be evaluated. The present clergy appraisal schemes in use in almost all dioceses in the Church of England would need to be integrated into this process. Review would need to involve those involved in the parish, including clergy, and 'outside' reviewers approved by the bishop. There would be no separate clergy appraisal/review process, though this would not preclude clergy having their own work consultants or advisory groups.

6. New appointments must be made on the basis of past evaluations

This provision indicates that future allocations of resources to the parish, including appointments of staff, should reflect the findings of the periodic reviews. It also indicates that staff applying for new appointments would need to disclose the findings of evaluations in their previous parishes. This would allow for people to build upon identified strengths in ministry; but would also prevent people who had shown lack of ability in certain areas of ministry from being able to conceal this in applying for new posts.

7. Clergy and others are encouraged to develop skills which are externally validated

It is important that clergy, like other workers, should have their skills recognised by properly approved bodies to ensure parity between different jobs and types of work. Such a process would also help in recognising and evaluating skills gained in work outside the Church's ministry, as noted in 1 above. In-service training provision should also move towards some structure of external validation.

These proposals are no panacea; but most of them, with the possible exception of 7, could be implemented without undue delay because they build upon processes and practices, like mission/social audits and clergy appraisal schemes, which already exist. These processes would require some adaptation, but the principles on which they operate are becoming part of the structures of the Church of England. The main question in all this is whether those who presently operate the structures of appointments, or those who benefit from their vagueness and lack of critical evaluation, are willing to contemplate such a change.

It is also important to stress that these ideas are both possible, as John Reader's account of applying the mission/social audit process to a group of Shropshire parishes testifies;[16] and also that they honour the reality of pastoral care, as Stephen Pattison suggests:

> The norm for thinking about pastoral care must now
> be that of the ordinary, non-trained, non-professional

person. Most people are primarily cared for, not by professionals or organisations such as churches, but by their families, friends and relatives. Often, they do not need highly specialised skills or a particular attitude on the part of their carers, but they do need constancy, availability and appropriateness. While there clearly is a role for professional or paid carers designated and trained as such, it is a mistake to see this latter kind of care as the norm. Indeed, regarding it in this way is a usurpation of power and significance which leads to an ideological distortion of reality.[17]

Nor is this a case of churches having to devote time to organisational questions to the detriment of caring for those in need. As Ann Morisy has argued, breaking down the old individualistic ways of working and seeking partnership with others in a process which is fully aware of the context of people's lives can enhance Christians' abilities to care and help.[18]

To criticise the liberal/rational view of education is not to deny that the ideal of people who learn because they wish to satisfy a burgeoning curiosity, or because they are open to new ideas, or because they are thoughtful and reflective about what they do and why, is an attractive one which ought to be dear to the hearts of all Christians, lay or ordained. Unfortunately this kind of attitude cannot be relied upon as the sole motivation and, if the church is not to become increasingly inward-looking, needs to be bolstered by other encouragement.

Ultimately, however, self-motivation will still be important in a process such as this, where considerable responsibility must be placed on the shoulders of parish clergy. The significance of structural changes like those proposed here is that they attempt to relocate the ministry of the clergy within the witness of the Church in a particular location rather than allowing it to be semi-independent of it, as seems often to be the case now. Clergy must be put into situations where the ability for sustained work with others is the norm, not simply an optional extra. There is no denying that this will press people towards a fundamentally different understanding of pastoral ministry from what has been taken as the norm since at least the middle of the nineteenth century. But without this, the churches, ever more dependent on diminishing numbers of clergy, face a bleak future.

FINALLY . . .

. . . another story which I hope returns this discussion to where it started, considering how people can work together effectively in a common enterprise. This is an extract from Alan Bennett's diaries:

> *27 June.* To a recording session at the BBC to lay down tracks for a short film I have written about Proust, *102 Boulevard Haussmann.* The Delmé Quartet play extracts from the César Franck String Quartet and the Fauré Piano Quartet, both possible models for the Vinteuil sonata that recurs in *A la Recherche.* Striking about the musicians is their total absence of self-importance. They play a passage, listen to it back, then give each other notes, and run over sections again. George Fenton, who is co-ordinating the music, also chips in, but he's a musician. David H., the director, chips in too, but he isn't a musician, just knows what atmosphere he wants at various points in the film. In the finish even I chip in, just because I know what I like. And the musicians nod and listen, try out a few bars here and there, then settle down and have another go. Now one could never do this with actors. No actor would tolerate a fellow performer who ventured to comment on what he or she was doing – comment of that sort coming solely from the director, and even

then it has to be carefully packaged and seasoned with plenty of love and appreciation. Whereas these players, all of them first-class, seem happy to listen to the views of anyone if it results in them doing a better job.[19]

So are clergy musicians or actors?

NOTES

1 Much of this way of training is embodied in the concept of the 'Learning Organisation'; for which see M. Pedler, J. Burgoyne and T. Boydell, *The Learning Company: a Strategy for Sustainable Development*, McGraw Hill (1997); also, Robin Greenwood, *Practising Community: the Task of the Local Church*, London, SPCK (1996).

2 Charles Handy, *Inside Organisations*, London, BBC Books (1990), p. 7.

3 Jeffrey Cox, *The English Churches in a Secular Society; Lambeth 1870-1930*, London, Oxford University Press (1982).

4 He failed.

5 On this, see my article 'Forty Years On: two clerical manuals' in *Modern Churchman*, new series, vol. 33, no. 2 (1991), pp. 30-36.

6 For more on this, see Gabriel Hebert, *Liturgy and Society*, London, Faber & Faber (1935), and Peter J. Jagger, *A History of the Parish and People Movement*, London, The Faith Press (1980).

7 David Clark, *A Survey of Christians at Work and its Implications for the Churches*, Birmingham, Westhill College in connection with the Christians in Public Life Programme (1993), pp. 15 f.

8 Section 2 of the Parochial Church Councils (Powers) Measure 1956, as amended by Section 6 of the Synodical Government Measure (1969).

9 A much more detailed treatment of this question is given in Stephen Pattison, *Pastoral Care and Liberation Theology*, London, SPCK (1997).

10 This is similar to Erving Goffman's observation that in 'total institutions' systems of privileges might also double as systems of punishment. See *Asylums*, Harmondsworth, Pelican Books (1968), pp. 51 ff.

11 For a detailed account of NOS see Roland Howard, *The Rise and Fall of the Nine O'clock Service*, London, Mowbray (1996).

12 Interestingly, investigations into the recent loss of £800,000,000 from the Church Commissioners' investment portfolio have revealed a similar lack of supervision in the financial management of the Church. See Terry Lovell, *Number One Millbank: the Financial Downfall of the Church of England*, London, HarperCollins (1997).

13 Quoted in H. G. G. Herklots, James Whyte and Robin Sharp, *Preparing for the Ministry of the 1970s*, London, SCM Press (1964), p. 29.

14 See, for example, Clement F. Rogers, *Pastoral Theology and the Modern World*, London, Oxford University Press (1920).

15 Andrew Bowden, *Ministry in the Countryside: a Model for the Future*, London, Mowbray (1994), p.132.

16 John Reader, *Local Theology: Church and Community in Dialogue*, London, SPCK (1994).

17 Stephen Pattison, *A Critique of Pastoral Care*, London, SCM Press, second edition (1993), p. 194.

18 Ann Morisy, *Beyond the Good Samaritan: Community Ministry and Mission*, London, Mowbray (1997).

19 Alan Bennett, *Writing Home*, London, Faber & Faber (1994), pp. 189 f.

APPENDIX 1

Questions used in the interviews

PART 1
Questions to Directors of Ordinands [see Chapter 2]

THE CURACIES

How are candidates 'matched' to curacies?

What assumptions are made about what people will have gained from the training process?

What decides numbers of curacies to be offered each year?

How are the competing claims of different parishes compared and a decision made which will have a curate?

How does the diocese decide who will be released?

How does the diocese decide to offer a job to a candidate it has not sponsored in training?

TRAINING INCUMBENTS

What qualities are looked for in 'training incumbents'?

Are there differences between incumbents for deacons and those for second curates?

How are training incumbents selected and trained?

How is ministry development monitored in the early years?

How does this relate to POT and later CME?

How are difficulties between incumbent and curate identified and addressed?

How are the findings of the early years identified and used in people's developing ministries?

PART 2
Questions for Curates

1. ATTITUDES TO PRESENT (OR PREVIOUS[1]) MINISTERIAL POST

1.1   What do you most enjoy about your present job?

1.2   What do you least enjoy about your present job?

1.3   Have you always felt this way about it? How has it changed?

1.4   What factors led you to accept this job?

Did the DDO, the bishop or any member of the diocesan staff suggest to you that you were particularly suited to the job?

Did you look at other jobs before deciding to accept this one?

1.5   Did you have any misgivings about this job when you accepted it? What were they?

2. GROWTH IN MINISTERIAL EXPERIENCE

2.1 Can you recall your feelings and experiences when you were first ordained? What were they?

2.2 What particular experiences first made you feel you were regarded by others as a minister? When did they happen?

2.3 What particular experiences first helped you to see yourself as a minister? When did they happen?

2.4 What sort of experiences (past or present) make you doubt yourself as a minister?

2.5 Have you ever thought you made a mistake by being ordained? Why?

3. PROFESSIONAL MENTORS, HELPERS AND SUPPORTERS

3.1 How did your relationship with your first incumbent develop? What were its good and bad features?

3.2 How did you get on with other colleagues (if any)?

3.3 How helpful were other ministers in enabling you to develop as a minister in your own right?

3.4 How helpful were senior clergy (bishops, archdeacons, etc.) and 'official' education and training programmes in helping you develop as a minister?

3.5 Who has/have been most helpful and supportive to you in your ministry so far?

4. FAMILY, FRIENDS AND FINANCE

4.1 Did the way/s your closest family and friends perceive and relate to you change when you were first ordained? How?

4.2 Have your family relationships or friendships been affected in other ways? How?

4.3 What material difference did your being ordained make to you and your family?

4.4 How has being ordained affected your material well-being and security?

4.5 Does your being a minister affect your ability to form new friendships or other relationships? How?

5. THE FUTURE

5.1 How do you hope your ministry might develop in the future? Do you think this is likely?

5.2 How has your view of, and attitude towards, the church developed since ordination?

5.3 Do you wish to add anything else?

NOTE

1 Because for those in a second appointment the questions referred to their first curacy.

APPENDIX 2

Statistical information from the work survey in Chapter 3

When the minimum time given to an activity is nil, the figure in brackets is the lowest reported time actually spent on it.

The nature of the survey meant that in some weeks some respondents had not undertaken a particular activity; this does not indicate that they never did so.

Because insufficient people were involved in categories O, DD to HH and JJ, these figures are not counted towards the results given in the table in Chapter 3. Categories II and KK are calculated within the interviewees' overall working day.

TABLE 1: TIME SPENT ON MINISTERIAL TASKS

		Hours per week		
Code	Task	Max.	Min.	Ave.
A	Conducting regular public worship	13.5	3.0	8.5
B	Conducting Rites of Passage	3.5	nil (1.0)	1.5
C	Participation in public worship, not as leader or preacher	10.0	nil (2.0)	3.5
D	Home visiting in connection with Rites of Passage	7.5	nil (1.0)	1.5
E	Home visiting for other specific purposes (not Rites of Passage)	10.5	nil (1.0)	3.0
F	General home visiting	7.5	nil (1.0)	1.5
G	Work with children in day school	8.0	nil (1.0)	1.0
H	Other work with children or young people	7.0	nil (1.0)	2.0

		Hours per week		
Code	Task	Max.	Min.	Ave.
I	Work with children or adults in preparation for Rites of Passage	2.5	nil (1.5)	0.5
J	Work with adult study or prayer groups	5.5	nil (2.0)	1.0
K	Work with other church adult groups	9.0	nil (1.0)	1.5
L	Work with non-church adult groups	2.5	nil (1.0)	0.5
M	Work with individuals in counselling or listening	4.5	nil (0.5)	1.5
N	Pastoral care of people outside home [eg. in hospital]	4.5	nil (1.0)	1.5
O	Pastoral work as chaplain (2 people)	8.0	2.0	n/a
P	Attending activities as a representative of the church	16.5	nil (2.0)	3.5
Q	Church Council (or sub-committees)	3.0	nil (2.0)	1.5
R	Meeting beyond the local church	8.5	nil (1.0)	1.5
S	Staff meetings	3.0	nil (1.0)	2.0
T	Planning worship (not preaching)	9.0	nil (1.0)	3.0
U	Planning preaching	9.0	nil (1.5)	3.5
V	Other planning meetings	3.5	nil (0.5)	1.5
W	Study for specific projects	7.5	nil (2.0)	1.5
X	Administration for Rites of Passage	4.0	nil (1.5)	2.0
Y	General church administration	12.0	1.0	4.5

		Hours per week		
Code	Task	Max.	Min.	Ave.
Z	Administration beyond local church	8.5	nil (1.0)	2.0
AA	General reading and study	9.5	nil (1.0)	2.0
BB	Personal spiritual reading	2.5	nil (0.5)	1.0
CC	Personal prayer and devotion	8.0	nil (0.5)	2.5
DD	Attending retreats/quiet days	nil	nil	n/a
EE	Appraisal/professional assessment	nil	nil	n/a
FF	Post-Ordination Training (4 people)	21.0	2.0	n/a
GG	Professional development with colleagues (2 people)	7.5	2.0	n/a
HH	Professional development not with colleagues (2 people)	3.0	1.5	n/a
II	Domestic tasks (e.g. shopping, meals)	31.0	1.5	14.0
JJ	Leisure in structured activities unconnected with church (3 people)	4.0	2.0	n/a
KK	Other time for recreation	13.5	nil (1.0)	5.5

APPENDIX 3

Notes on some other relevant surveys

1 BOOKS

There have been a number of books over the years which cover aspects of the work done by clergy, by no means all of them curates. These form the background to some of this research and where their findings have directly impinged upon it mention has been made in the notes at the end of each chapter. The following are a brief selection, with some introductory comments, though no doubt other material exists.

- Robert Towler and A. P. M. Coxon, *The Fate of the Anglican Clergy,* London, MacMillan (1979)

  A sociological study of ordinands and clergy. The use of material dating back to the 1960s meant that some aspects of the survey were dated when published, though there is still a good deal of useful information.

- Stewart Ranson, Alan Bryman and Bob Hinings, *Clergy, Ministers and Priests,* London, Routledge & Kegan Paul (1977)

  Another sociological study which, despite being published two years before Towler and Coxon, is possibly more current. This is a comparative study of Anglican, Methodist and Roman Catholic clergy and highlights some interesting comparisons between them.

- Anthony Russell, *The Clerical Profession,* London, SPCK (1980)

A further sociological study, though with a more historical perspective than the two previously cited. This traces the changes in the role of clergy in the Church of England during the nineteenth and twentieth centuries and discusses the clergy's adoption of the model of the professional person which developed in the same period. Originally the author's doctoral thesis.

- Mary Loudon, *Revelations; the Clergy Questioned,* London, Hamish Hamilton (1994)

  A series of interviews with Anglican clergy about their work. Very readable and informative.

- David Hare, *Asking Around; Background to the David Hare Trilogy,* London, Faber & Faber in association with the National Theatre (1993)

  Material from David Hare's research for his play *Racing Demon,* including interviews with clergy.

- Catherine Treasure, *Walking on Glass; Women Deacons Speak Out,* London, SPCK (1991)

  A series of interviews with women Deacons in the Church of England in the period before the General Synod's vote to allow women to be ordained as priests in 1992.

2 REPORTS

Two reports into ministers' experiences have also come to light in the last few years:

- Paul Ballard, Andrew Morton, Heather Snidle and Roger Young, *Voices from the Margin; the Non-Stipendiary Ministry in the Church in Wales,* Cardiff, Social and Pastoral Care

Unit, Department of Religious and Theological Studies, University of Wales Cardiff, Holi 7 (1996)

A report to the Archbishop and Bishops and the Provincial Board of Ministry of the Church in Wales by members of the Religious and Theological Studies Department at Cardiff University. It is of interest in that, despite focusing on a different group of clergy in another province of the Anglican Communion, there is a considerable similarity between its findings and those of my own research.

• Adrian Harbidge, *Those Whom DDO Hath Joined Together . . .* Privately published by the author (1996)

The outcome of a sabbatical study by the Vicar of Chandler's Ford, Hampshire, himself a training incumbent. He received 79 responses to his questionnaire to those who had been curates in 1991 and 92 responses from the same curates' training incumbents. Once again, despite different methodology, there is considerable similarity between his findings and mine; his research benefits from a larger sample and also comments from training incumbents. He noted:

Consultation between the incumbent and the diocese improves the chances of a successful curacy by 16 per cent.

Formal assessment of the progress of the training by the incumbent and the curate improves the chances of success by 30 per cent.

Formal assessment of the progress of the training by the diocese and the curate improves the chances of success by 39 per cent.

Copies were sent to all diocesan bishops and Directors of POT in the Church of England.

ACKNOWLEDGEMENTS

The publishers would like to thank the following for their permission to use copyright material in this book:

BBC Worldwide Ltd, 80 Wood Lane, London W12 0TT, for an extract from *Inside Organisations* by Charles Handy, © 1990 BBC Books.

Cassell plc, Wellington House, 125 Strand, London WC2R 0BB, for an extract from *Ministry in the Countryside: A Model for the Future* by Andrew Bowden, © 1994 Mowbray (an imprint of Cassell plc).

Faber & Faber Ltd, 3 Queen Square, London WC1N 3AU, for an extract from *Writing Home* by Alan Bennett, © 1994 Faber & Faber.

SCM Press Ltd, 9-17 St Albans Place, London N1 0NX, for extracts from *Preparing for the Ministry of the 1970s* by H. G. G. Herklots, James Whyte and Robin Sharp, © 1964 SCM Press; and *A Critique of Pastoral Care*, Second Edition, by Stephen Pattison, © 1993 SCM Press.